Mike Wood

HOW TO WIN?

How to Win?

Democratic planning and the abolition of unemployment. Some agreed principles, and some problems to be resolved.

Michael Barratt Brown
Tony Benn
Stephen Bodington
Ken Coates
Mike Cooley
Mike George
Stuart Holland
John Hughes
Michael Meacher
Alan Taylor

Edited by Ken Coates

Spokesman
for the Institute for Workers' Control

First published in 1981 by Spokesman, for the Institute for Workers' Control, Bertrand Russell House, Gamble Street, Nottingham NG7 4ET.

Cloth ISBN 0 85124 329 0
Paper ISBN 0 85124 330 4

Printed by the Russell Press Ltd., Nottingham

Contents

CHAPTER ONE

Introduction

Ken Coates

Dreadful. That is the universal description of Britain's crisis of unemployment, the worst in our entire history. Even the British press, not notably devoted to the pursuit of truth, is compelled to register some hints of the calamity which has befallen us.The statistics, and the trends they reveal, are so awesome that they defy concealment.

With rising three million workless victims already, the Manpower Services Commission informed us in the first half of 1981 that we must expect the numbers to increase still further for at least two more years, and to remain at similar levels for four. The MSC reported also that the direct cost of this profound malaise to the Exchequer has already passed £7 billion annually. This burden takes count solely of taxes forfeited by the revenue and disbursements from social security funds. Assessment of the cost of lost production is more difficult, but cautious estimates put it at not less than £10 billion each year. Other estimates than those of the MSC are higher on all counts. But whatever the actual cost of the damage may be in global terms, its specific effects on people and their districts are already all-too-apparent.

Unemployment hits hardest at young people, women and black people. The length of exposure to it inevitably increases as the absolute numbers of workless increase. More and more people are deprived of jobs, not merely for weeks, but for months and even years. Regional variations add especial burdens in the worst hit areas. Already there are whole zones of blight, in which entire populations are trapped in profound crisis. Some towns endure percentages of workless people which, if generalised, would imply 5,000,000, even 6,000,000 people on the dole nationally. And the worst news is that a moderate recovery would displace more jobs still, as investment picked up to the point were micro-chips could begin to displace people on an ever-widening scale. The scale of recovery which could solve this problem by engendering an explosion of new demand has boggled the minds of all those who have seriously tried thinking it through.

The threat which all this poses to democratic institutions is sharp and deep. It is quite unimaginable that free trade unions and parliamentary democracy will be able to survive in prolonged exposure to this degree of paralysis. There are menacing precedents in the experience of the inter-war slump, which experience has already been surpassed in severity by our present trauma. We have every reason for alarm, and every need for a considered and rational response. The defence of democracy in such bleak conditions is only possible as a result of its extension. This is not an easy process, and it will always be misrepresented by those interests which suffer from it. But the simple test which working people will put to it is, how far does it restore the right to work?

None of this is new, and the Institute for Workers' Control has been campaigning about it continuously for several years, since the inauguration of its Full Employment Campaign immediately after the last visit of the International Monetary Fund to the policy tables of Government in Britain during the Labour administration. Over and again we and others have insisted that public expenditure, far from shrinking, should expand; that new manufacturing jobs are capital-intensive, whilst the personal social services are labour intensive; that trade, far from prospering in the framework of the European Community, must be planned in a complementary way with a whole range of other partners in order to prevent the wholesale destruction of British industry. The Full Employment Campaign attracted support from major trade union leaders, from a large number of Members of Parliament, from distinguished scholars and from working people in many widely different sectors of the economy. But the fall of the Labour Government in 1979 testified to the fact that policies were not modified in time. Various Labour budgets, and related economic initiatives, contributed to the abandonment of full employment as the sacred priority of the Labour Party. The defeat of the Government was in such circumstances entirely predictable. But before it fell, it had prepared public thinking for the unthinkable. Mrs Thatcher's relentless monetarism could not have been tolerated for one second if Denis Healey had not prepared the field for her.

However, on Labour's front benches nobody nowadays admits to once kissing hands with the IMF. In these more cataclysmic days our cities burn and fight. De-industrialisation, the collapse of one sector after another of manufacturing industry, has reached epidemic proportions. More and more equipment is sold at a tithe of its value to competitors overseas, as the liquidators work over-time. Recovery recedes with every sale. We have documented the extent of this disastrous evolution in a companion volume to this one, by John Hughes.[1] This book offers a range of attempts to chart a different path. Some of its prescriptions are consensual for all its contributors, but it is evident that there remain problems on which they disagree. Parts of these disagreements will remain, because they reflect unavoidable differences of emphasis which will continue to need expression within the Labour movement throughout the difficult period it is now entering. Other areas of disagreement will need to be resolved in the very near future, and their clear statement is the first step to such resolution. What is perfectly plain is that, far from entering a period of monolithic and monotonous dogma, Labour is embarking upon a vital discussion, which faces some classic problems of socialist theory in a complete-ly novel context, and at the same time encounters a daunting range of new problems for which there are no established precedents.

Upon a number of key prescriptions, however, there is powerful pressure for agreement.

There are three linked levels at which the Labour movement must elaborate a strategy for recovery, remembering always that this will be inordinately difficult, since Mrs Thatcher's administration will, as Tony Benn never tires of reminding us, have devastated more British factories than were lost in Goering's blitz.

A new Labour Government will need to be able to cope at the in-ternational level, in a climate in which British competitive capacity will be at an all-time low and, in which there will indeed be unknown new hazards arising from the announced policies of President Reagan. Labour will also need to provide a national framework for recovery, at the intermediary level. And at the local level, it will need to stimulate a vast effort of municipal and co-operative industry, in order to get the country back to work.

To set the problem in this focus, we need to see the necessary na-tional policies precisely as "intermediary", capable of stimulating activity by the people, and capable of holding back, and with effort and skill, overcoming, the international pressures which will other-wise stifle such activity. In the past, Labour Party programmes have seen their national policy commitments as central, and their international and local options as decidedly secondary. But in the middle 'eighties this will be completely impossible. An interna-tional effort is needed to fight back against monetarism, to defeat

militarism, and to control the transnational corporations. As far as
the trade unions are concerned, shorter working time and the
humane control of new technologies are matters requiring international agreement and co-ordinated action. And for the present
commitments of the Labour movement, the separation of Britain
from its adherence to the Treaty of Rome positively requires a
carefully thought out plan for international trade, not only in
respect of short-term protection, where this is relevant, but much
more in pursuit of that new world economic order which has been a
constant theme of third world governments in the United Nations
and elsewhere. All these issues will be vitally important to any
government which seriously intends to restore full employment.

At local level, municipal and co-operative development will need
official encouragement and funding, and a whole batch of enabling
measures will thus become essential. The Lucas Aerospace initiative, in which the workers drew up their own elaborate proposals for maintaining work on a very wide range of useful projects, in opposition to redundancies, will need imitators on every
side, but these imitators will need to meet official support rather
than passivity or downright hostility. Local planning, involving the
unions in their own most primary organisations, will take on a
crucial dimension. The national measures which will allow state
economic intervention to function appropriately will thus involve a
completely new range of concerns, and will be inconceivable within
a constrained bureaucratic structure.

Because it is predominantly concerned with the reconquest of full
employment, this book only treats other key matters tangentially.
The effect of slump, however, drastically augments military
threats: not only do beleaguered governments find external adver-
saries convenient bogeys with which to frighten their citizens, but
the temptation to militarism and authoritarianism is part of a
deeper irrationalism which has recurred throughout modern history
on every reappearance of prolonged economic crisis. Of course,
military spending intensifies the problems which give rise to it. But
today this phenomenon is more frightening than ever it has been
before: the wars which fell on mankind after previous similar experiences took dreadful toll, but the war in current preparation
would be the ultimate cataclysm. We have confronted the problems
involved in this in another book published alongside this one, and
are bound to refer interested readers to that, simply because
coherent presentation of the arguments involved would double the
length of this particular work.[2]

Yet the problem exists, and requires an international response by the Labour movement. The most promising beginnings of such a response are to be found in the growing commitment to European Nuclear Disarmament, which seeks to create a nuclear-weapons-free zone in the political territory of Europe. This would, once achieved, spell the autonomy of Europe from bloc politics. The struggle for such policies, even while it falls short of achieving them, creates a growing pressure for non-alignment in Europe, which in turn makes possible the increasing autonomy of the European working-class movement. It is necessary to set out the reasoning which supports this process, and this task will be a priority one for socialists during the next months. Evidently neither American nor Soviet patronage of the European trade unions and political parties has anything but trouble to offer the working people of Europe. The vicissitudes of superpower influence and intrigue in post-war Europe are complex. Here, it is simply necessary to say that the effort to recover the freedom of independent action by the workers of Europe has its economic and industrial aspects as well as its obvious implications for the disarmament campaign. These aspects are not reducible to the issues at stake in the existing economic institutions of Europe, whether in the EEC or in Comecon. Because there already exists a non-aligned Europe, containing such powerful socialist forces as the Austrian, Swedish and Finnish Labour movements, and the self-management experiments of Yugoslavia, there already exists a potential focus for alternative links which will begin to change the options open to other Europeans. Already the socialist and eurocommunist parties in Greece and Spain show considerable awareness of these issues. The adoption of more radical policies in many European socialist organisations, the victory of Mitterand in France, and the rise of Solidarity in Poland; all offer new openings, even though in each case there are unresolved tensions which express serious difficulties. Similarly, the evolution of Eurocommunism removes many obstacles to the ultimate reunification of the mass European Labour movement, at the same time that it reflects some of the still unresolved problems we must all face, whether we approach them separately or together.

British socialist policy should clearly seek to develop all these affinities, as a deliberate part of an attack on the disastrous legacy of capitalism in our island. And yet, while the recovery of fully autonomous action by European Labour will be a great conquest, enabling the true interests of our working people to achieve rational expression, it will not be a sufficient conquest, unless it is also founded on a profoundly international commitment.

The diagnoses of the "North-South" schism by the Brandt commission have aroused widespread concern in all the European states, because under-development now takes the form of ever more open and intractable crisis. Starvation is a growing problem in whole global zones. Numerous States in the third world cannot even meet the burden of the interest payments on their accumulated debts. The slump threatens ever deeper crisis to the peoples of such areas. Their difficulties aggravate the slump. Unfortunately, the prescriptions of Brandt's Report are not apposite to meet the conditions it describes. As Algeria's founding President Ben Bella said, when he visited London in July 1981, "there is no North-South dialogue: there is a North-South monologue". Keynesian remedies for world poverty can never be implemented by those powerful states which have already repudiated them for their own use.

Yet the recovery of British industry can only be adequately postulated within this international perspective, and since Brandt's programme will not be effectively implemented, Britain's intervention requires a rapid development of the kinds of thinking outlined in Michael Barratt Brown's consideration of trade policy below.

As is so often the case, solidarity set within such a field of choices becomes joint and reciprocal support, not simply disinterested generosity.

This argument about a new internationalism keys into our treatment of local enterprise and decentralised planning in Britain itself, about which we offer a variety of views, all of which are adamant that no central bureaucracy can write Britain back to work by means of blueprints and exhortations. The central institutions of planning and economic initiative which we seek at the intermediate (National) level must by common consent be seen as a catalyst to local initiative and democratic actions. This they cannot be if they are powerless, because the inhibitors of all such action are numerous, well understood, and, in crisis Britain, more powerful than ever they have been. Yet the power of such national planning bodies will, ultimately, rest on the democratic forces they serve, or on nothing.

We could explain this problem away by abstract formulae about decentralisation, but this would be a disservice, because it would obscure the most difficult problems without resolving them. Of course, there is a verbal trick in the argument which is all too often ignored: decentralisation entails the existence of a centre, and normally implies a change of local relationships with it rather than an annulment of them. Bitter lessons have been learnt about the follies of unaccountable planning. Accountable planning, however, has not yet been seriously tried. In all their diversity these essays seek to explore the kinds of institutions it will need.

The debate within the Labour movement during the late nineteen seventies raised many crucial issues about political organisation. All of these are burningly relevant to the political economy of the late 'eighties. Their resolution is a task for a vast movement of people, not for a cabal of scholars. These people will be taking part in a transformation with implications for an area far wider than the geography of one small rainy island. All the signs are that the size of the challenge will condition the scope of the response.

Footnotes

1. *Britain in Crisis: Deindustrialisation and how to fight it* by John Hughes, Spokesman, 1981.
2. *The Dynamics of European Nuclear Disarmament* by Alva Myrdal and Others, Spokesman, 1981.

CHAPTER TWO

International Workers' Plans: Foreign Trade and Investment in the British Economy

Michael Barratt Brown

Introduction

Any strategy for rebuilding the British economy based upon national planning, workers' plans and municipal enterprise, must have an international dimension. Britain is an island, but unchangeably built into the structure of the world economy. This is not a matter for despair but for positive action. When the General Electric Company plants in Merseyside were threatened with closure in 1969 and the first work-in was under discussion by the workers, Institute for Workers' Control members wrote letters to a number of Third World country embassies in London, asking them whether they had any interest in the electrical equipment produced at these works, and if so, what government trading arrangements would be needed to facilitate the placing of orders. Replies were received from several embassies all expressing interest, but making it clear that their countries would have to find new markets in Britain for their products so as to be able to pay for the products of the GEC works. Workers' Plans in Britain have in effect to be complemented by International Workers' Plans. It is to the urgent need of relating measures taken in Britain to the solidarity of workers here and elsewhere, and especially in the developing countries of the Third World, that this contribution is directed.

Britain's Historic Trade Pattern

The British economy has historically been closely integrated into the capitalist world economy. Over 25% of Britain's national product has always been exported. This puts Britain in the same class as much smaller countries like Canada, New Zealand, Belgium and the Netherlands, and is in sharp contrast with the position in the USA, France, Italy or Japan, where exports have never made up more than around 10% of the national product. Foreign trade is thus of crucial importance for Britain's economic recovery. Britain established itself as the "workshop of the world" in the nineteenth century as the result of British capital imposing a quite artificial division of labour in the world capitalist system. British industry supplied manufactured goods in exchange for food and raw materials from the rest of the world. As short a time ago as the late 1960s import penetration of the British market by foreign manufactures was far lower than today and the total of finished and semi-manufactured goods made up no more than 40% of all UK imports but over 85% of all exports. Today they almost balance: 64% of imports and 74% of exports are manufactured goods. Trade in fuels does in fact balance so that as much as 13% of all UK imports are now paid for by North Sea Oil (see Table 1).

There are long historical trends here that cannot easily be changed. First, owners of capital in all those countries that succeeded Britain in industrial development sought to establish a similar place in the world market for their manufactured goods — the USA, France, Germany, Japan, Italy. British industry lost its monopoly of world trade in manufactures a hundred years ago. In these other countries, however, while the pattern of exports of manufactures and imports of food and raw materials was similar, foreign trade was, as we have stated, a smaller part of total output than in the case of Britain. Secondly, trade between the industrialised capitalist countries themselves has steadily grown as a proportion of total world trade and particularly of the trade in manufactured goods. By the 1960s over a half of all world trade was flowing between the industrialised capitalist countries and much the greater part of this consisted of manufactured goods. The huge rise in oil prices after 1973, however, checked this tendency and re-established the importance of the non-industrialised countries in world trade. Thirdly, a steadily increasing proportion of all international trade is carried on in the form of transfers inside the giant transnational companies. It is estimated that nearly a half of both UK imports and exports are transfers of this sort. Fourthly, the establishment of the European Community as a Common Market without internal tariffs, and Britain's entry into the Market, have served to switch Britain's trade from its traditional pattern of the exchange of British manufactures for overseas food and raw materials.

Rising Import Penetration and the Response of Exports

Does it matter then that imports are now providing a larger proportion of the UK market for manufactures and that these are being paid for with the earnings from North Sea oil? The answer is that it certainly does: firstly, because North Sea oil only lasts for about another 30 years and it would then be difficult to revive home-based industries whose output had been replaced by imported goods; secondly, because the only reason why imports were not larger in 1980, and the UK balance of trade was even in surplus, was that the whole British economy had been cut back in that year. As a result of rising unemployment, consumers' purchasing power was reduced and as a result of that less finished goods were imported by consumers and less raw materials and semi-manufactures were imported by industry. As soon as the economy is expanded again, as Labour's alternative economic strategy proposes, there is no doubt that imports will rise sharply and well in excess of exports unless measures are taken to prevent this.

It appears from a comparison of the figures for UK imports as a proportion of home demand for manufactures and the figures for exports as a proportion of UK manufactured output, that exports have kept up with imports quite satisfactorily in the last decade (see Table 2). The only reason why this so-called "success" has been possible is that imports have been held back and the home market for manufactured output has been depressed by Government cuts. Consumers' expenditure in 1980 was still only 7% above the level in 1973 and is not expected to rise in 1981 or 1982. The resulting check to the rise in imports has been combined with an improvement in the UK terms of trade (the value of imports that can be bought with UK exports — see Table 3) to make it possible by 1980 for exports to establish an actual trade surplus. This is revealed in Table 4 which shows up very well in the balance of trade for particular commodities the third problem involved in the process of permitting a steady rise in the import proportion of the British market for manufactures. This is that while UK deficits on food, beverages and tobacco, on basic materials and above all on fuels, have nowhere near risen in line with export prices, the favourable balances on manufactures have not risen with export prices either. This is particularly true of finished manufactures where the favourable balance in the *value* of exports over imports in 1980 was less than a fifth of the export value, whereas in 1970 it was over a half of the export value. The fourth reason for worry is that British industrial output is being cut back far more sharply than is the case in the rest of the capitalist world. Far from Britain sharing in a world recession, which is the view often presented by the Thatcher Government, Britain is in fact having a major recession while the rest of the world suffers only a slowing down in the rate of growth (see table 5).

Finally, the imbalance of UK trade with the EEC, which was running at an average of some £2.500 millions a year from 1975 to 1979, while it was corrected in 1980, seems likely to reappear in 1981. And this trade figure takes no account of the levies of some £1000 million paid to the EEC on account of British purchases of non-EEC agricultural products. Most serious is the trade diversion effect of Britain's entry into the EEC. The concentration of UK purchases upon the Common Market — shown in Table 6, rising from 27% in 1970 to 42% in 1980, has, at least temporarily, undermined trade relations with other producers, particularly of food and raw materials in the developing countries. It is once again only the holding down of the volume of imports that has enabled exports to cover imports from the EEC. Exporting to the EEC means that the UK competes with manufactured products which are the stock-in-trade of the EEC countries themselves. The loss of trade with developing countries means that the flows of trade are running far below their optimum. The developing countries could sell more to Britain if they were encouraged by long term contracts. They could then afford to buy more from Britain.

Apart from the depressed level of demand in the UK leading to lower imports, two other factors have temporarily reduced the deficit in Britain's trade with the EEC. The first was the high value of sterling in relation to other European currencies during 1980. The other, and main, reason for the surplus was greatly increased exports of oil from the North Sea. In 1980 these were valued at £2660 million. The 1980 balance of trade in manufactures showed a deficit of £1700 million, leaving deficits with West Germany, France and Italy being somewhat offset by positive balances with Eire and the Netherlands (see Table 6).

Britain's Trading Partners — Leaving the EEC

The picture then of UK trade since Britain entered the European community is of a twofold shift, from exchanges of manufactures for food and raw materials with developing countries, to mutual exchange of manufactured goods within the *developed* countries. Competition becomes sharper in the markets of the developed countries while the share in the world trade of the developing countries declines apart from trade with the oil producers. The EEC in 1980 supplied over 50% of Britain's manufactured imports (Table 6) and took about 40% of UK manufactured exports. If the British economy were to be expanded, the deficit on this trade could easily grow very much wider, even than the £1700 million recorded in 1980. This is the major argument for a Labour Government imposing import controls. There are several major objections which are put forward against the imposition of import controls:

1. Import controls are not permitted under the free trade provisions of the EEC's Rome Treaty and whether we withdrew or were expelled, British controls would be subject to retaliation by the EEC and other major trading partners like the USA.
2. Import controls would mean UK consumers paying higher prices for British manfactures and UK producers being feather-bedded and failing to reduce costs and improve quality and service when protected from competition.
3. Import controls mean, in effect, exporting unemployment to other countries and protecting British workers at the expense of workers elsewhere and especially those in the Third World.
4. Import controls put into the hands of Government officials a range of powers to discriminate between companies and industries, by rationing limited supplies of imports, which will inevitably benefit larger established companies at the expense of smaller and younger enterprises (war time controls were actually operated by the giant companies).

The general argument employed against all these objections is that import controls do not mean a reduction of imports *below* current levels, held down as they are by deflationary policies, but only a measure of restriction on the *growth* of imports as the economy is reflated. Nothing could be more damaging to other countries' trade, in particular to the Third World countries, as well as to the efficiency of British manufacturers, than the current low level of purchasing power in the UK.

This argument is an important one, but I do not consider that it is a sufficient response to the objections raised. In the first instance there is the question of EEC membership. There can be little doubt that the response of the other EEC countries to UK import controls will not be concerned so much with loss of market shares as with Britain's breaking of the capitalist rules of the game. The question has then to be faced of Britain leaving the Community, either by withdrawal or by expulsion; but more than this it involves the whole relationship of the British economy to the giant transnationals. We will take the two issues in turn.

What is the alternative to the current heavy concentration of Britain's trade on the EEC? There would be a number of major advantages deriving from withdrawal or expulsion. The first would be release from the Common Agricultural Policy and this would have three advantages: the possibility of obtaining cheaper food, the removal of the £1000 million contribution to the EEC budget, above all the freedom to make long-term agreements with trading partners to plan trade exchanges, including contracts for food and raw material purchases in exchange for sales of manufactured goods. The main fear that is expressed about the consequences of leaving the EEC is that, even if imports from the EEC could thereafter be controlled, there would be instant retaliation against UK exports. If nothing else, the 10% external EEC tariff would be raised against British goods and other discriminating measures might be applied. These would depend very much on the policies of the giant transnational companies operating in Britain and Europe whose trading activities we shall examine in a moment. The 10% tariff would undoubtedly be an obstacle to trade, but it should be put into the context of the 25% loss of competitiveness of British goods over the last two years during the rise in the value of the £ sterling against other European currencies. Although this loss was a serious one for British exporters, it did not lead to an actual fall in the volume of UK non-oil exports to the EEC but only to an increase in real terms in the deficit in 1979 which was rectified in 1980. The special reasons for the overall improvement in UK trade performance with the EEC have already been mentioned — high value of the £, reduced import demand, growing oil sales.

The most important fact in Britain's trade in manufactures, revealed with great clarity in Table 7, is that while the deficit in UK trade with the EEC continues, there is a considerable and sustained UK surplus in trade with the rest of the world. It is this which British exporters would have to build on in making good any losses sustained by withdrawal from the Common Market. UK trade with the developed countries of the world, even outside the EEC, is always in deficit. But this is in large part because of Britain's major purchases of grains and basic materials from these countries. It is with the oil exporting countries and other *under*developed economies that Britain's trade is strongest (Table 8). To develop this trade, however, at least with the non-oil producers, means planning for expanded purchases from them in place of current dependence on EEC supplies. Such planning can only be looked at in the light, not only of EEC restrictions, but of the powerful control that the transnational companies have now over the greater part of international trade flows.

Transnational companies' movements of goods and capital

To judge by the full page advertisements placed in the press by the giant transnational companies during the 1975 referendum campaign on Britain's membership of the EEC, the EEC membership is

of great importance for their activities. This is because the rules of
the EEC provide for free movement both of goods and capital
throughout the Community. One of the results of Britain's entry
and the Government's subsequent relaxation of exchange controls,
has been a steady flow of investment out of the UK and into North
West Europe. Despite the fact that income flowing into Britain
from UK owned property abroad has in recent years barely covered
income paid abroad to foreign owners of property in Britain, the
figures for net UK investment abroad have been on a rising trend.
In other words, new capital has been invested overseas rather than
in Britain. Transnational companies have been increasingly
transferring operations from the UK to Europe and North
America. It is well known that this has often been done by means of
transfer pricing — high prices being charged for imports from
foreign plants into British plants, low prices when components
move the other way — so that losses were made in Britain and profits were made overseas where taxes were lower. Most British based
transnationals now produce more overseas than in Britain. A Bank
of England *Quarterly Bulletin* put the position quite squarely:

"UK companies are planning to service their new or expanded
European markets mainly from continental bases. This, when
coupled with the evidence that continental firms are servicing
their UK markets more through exports than from production
facilities in the UK is somewhat discouraging for the future
growth of the UK economy . . .

There have been sharp increases in *net* direct UK investment in
Western Europe and North America during the 1970s, escecially
in high technology sectors. There appear also to have been
substantial divestments, in the early part of the decade, by
multinationals in the UK, particularly by those of US origin . . .
The observed changes in trade performanc≥ may well reflect
these developments."

('UK Manufacturing Industry: international integration and
trade performance,' Panic and Joyce, *Bank of England
Quarterly Bulletin,* March 1980)

All this provides further reasons for a Labour Government
regaining control over capital movements and re-establishing
manufacturing bases in Britain. What has to be taken into account,
however, is the very considerable difficulty for any government in
controlling capital movements that are effected through transfer
pricing of the movement of imports and exports. Some major companies will have to be brought into public ownership as part of any

alternative economic strategy but, short of bringing the British bases of all large transnationally operating companies into public ownership, the only effective means of control is through Planning Agreements signed between Government and company with trade union participation. The reason for this last provision is not in this instance my commitment to workers' control, but the absolute necessity, if governments are to take control of foreign trade out of the hands of the giant companies, that they must have available inside knowledge of what exactly is being transferred within giant companies when components and equipment move across national boundaries. Only trade union representatives with direct shop floor contacts can provide this, as Tony Benn found during his period of tenure at the Department of Industry. An essential part of Planning Agreements would then be the obligation on companies, not only to invest in Britain and expand exports from UK bases, but also a requirement on them to supply goods under contracts negotiated with foreign governments as part of long term agreements for expanded trade exchanges.

This is not the place to argue the general case for Planning Agreements, but their importance in a restructuring of Britain's foreign trade must be evident. The power of modern governments to influence large company decisions through powers to guarantee export credits, to make grants and loans, to offer tax concessions and infrastructural facilities, has never been in question. What British governments have singularly failed to do has been to use these powers to direct the owners and controllers of capital into activities that coincided with governments' own objectives. Since Planning Agreements will take time to be worked out — and they have never yet been attempted with non-nationalised companies in Britain since their removal from the Labour Government's armoury in 1975 with Tony Benn's transfer from the Department of Industry — government will have to establish Exchange Controls and temporary import quotas. The best way to do this would be by establishing a monopoly of foreign trade. This would mean that all major trade movements (above a certain value) had to be conducted through a department of foreign trade. Already all imports and exports are subject to customs, Export Credit guarantees and inland revenue and exchange control. It would only be necessary to add to these controls specific directions and limitations such as are operated in wartime for foreign trade to become a key sector of Government economic planning. In addition to its regulatory role, the Department could place orders on behalf of smaller firms both for imports and exports.

Planned Trade and Import Controls

The aim of this paper is to argue that import controls are not enough. The TUC and the Labour Party are both committed to a policy of imposing controls over imports and this policy has been extended into the concept of planned trade. Unfortunately the concept has remained undeveloped despite much discussion of it on Working Groups of the Labour Party's National Executive Committee. That the concept is even being discussed is a great advance. Proposals that I have been putting forward over 20 years for planning of foreign trade have been greeted with a quite shattering silence. Objections, when they can be brought into the open, range from a general scepticism about bringing any part of the transnational companies' operations under control, to quite specific doubts about the extent of bureaucratic interference that would be involved. The most serious objection probably arises from deep distrust of extending government powers and from recollections of the way the big companies moved into government departments during the Second World War to manage the rationing of scarce imports between rival claimants.

The concept of planned trade has, it must be said, to be protected from what it is *not*. First, it is *not* a proposal for crude barter arrangements between one country and another. Second, it is *not* a proposal for a bureaucratically controlled plan operated from above by some international institution like the United Nations to manage trade exchanges. Thirdly, it is *not* a plan for unaccountable allocation of imported supplies being fixed between giant companies. This means that what it should be is (a) a multilateral plan among several nations equally prepared to plan their trade; (b) one that is based on independent national plans which can be integrated by mutual agreement and (c) one that involves Parliamentary and Trade Union combine control over giant company decisions. It may seem that these requirements go beyond what is possible in a capitalist world political economy.

It must be said that those who criticise the failure of Keynesian national demand management in the current collapse into "stagflation", tend to forget that Keynes assumed not only national Government measures to sustain purchasing power at home, but also international measures to maintain *world* purchasing power. So long as gold flowed out from the United States to stimulate demand in the rest of the world, all was well. So long even as Eurodollars were acceptable as a world currency after the dollar could not be changed into gold i.e. from 1971, the United States could buy more that it sold and her purchases stimulated economic activity the world over. But when US war expenditures in Vietnam escalated and Japanese cars and German machines challenged United States products, then doubts arose in the minds of those with capital to invest concerning the dollar as the world's money. Investment went into giant tankers, into property and land, into gold (raising the price from $37.5 an ounce to over $600 an ounce) and finally into Government bonds at escalating rates of interest.

Keynes always understood that national government measures to support national purchasing power at home would need to be complemented by international agreement to support world demand. The relative decline of the sums available for international aid and investment combined with soaring oil prices have struck hard at world purchasing power outside the oil economies. World demand has been falling at a rate not seen since the 1930s. So far this decline does not seem so serious because it is only a decline from a high rate of *growth* achieved after 1945. But the cumulative effect of low economic growth rates must spell actual world slump at a later date. Before that happens, and it has not happened yet (see Table 5), what international measures can governments be expected to take to remedy, or try to remedy, the situation?

Of course it may be argued that the fact that none of Keynes' international requirements — automatic finance without strings from the IMF and massive loans from the World Bank — have been made available in the past, means that it is utopian to believe in them in the future. But human beings learn from the past, and pressure increases — witness first the Pearson Report and then the Brandt Report — from the most respectable circles (Willy Brandt, Ted Heath *et al)* for worldwide Keynesian demand management to increase the purchasing power of the poor. But it is put forward in a form that is most unlikely to work as a straight transfer of wealth through aid from rich to poor nations. It never has worked and is not likely to work, first, because the sums are inadequate and secondly becaust they go to the wrong people in the Third World — who salt them away in Swiss banks or property investment in the West End of London, New York or Brussels, or in prestige projects that do little to help real development.

In any case, almost every underdeveloped country, according to the Resolutions of the UN Conference on Trade and Development, would prefer more trade to more aid. This means that they could have built in some security of planned trade exchanges; for this is what they are looking for — a guarantee of purchase of certain quantities of their products over a period of years in exchange for the supply of the machinery and equipment that they need for their industrialisation programmes.

The present situation is that international trade is balanced well below the optimum level. Because of balance of payments deficits, one country cuts back its purchasing power and, therefore, the volume of its imports. Those imports are some other countries' exports and when they are cut back the other country, to balance its foreign payments, must reduce its imports. The cuts are cumulative on either side so that worldwide resources of industrial and agricultural production are operated below full capacity. The alternative is to reverse the spiral by developing co-operation between the advanced industrial countries and the backward countries struggling to develop their economies through a system of planned trade.

A New Proposal for Planned Trade

What is meant by planned trade? The proposal put forward here for inclusion in Labour Party programmes is that an incoming Labour Government should call upon all Britain's trading partners who were interested in planning their foreign trade to draw up an International Trade Plan. Each would indicate, item by item, the increases (and occasionally decreases) which they would hope to make in both their imports and exports over a period of years. These would be expressed in quantitative volume terms with suggested origins and destinations. When all the schedules had been prepared, they could be fed into a computer to discover where there were mismatches and where there were excesses of supply or demand. This information would be circulated to the participating governments with suggested alternatives for reconciling mismatches. After a number of runs and discussions between the several parties, an International Trade Plan would be drawn up. The status of the Plan would be as an indicative target rather than a mandatory requirement; but on its basis governments could sign contracts and encourage firms to make agreements to meet them. Clauses governing prices would be subject to annual revision.

If this proposal appears naive and utopian, with the implication that no governments would participate, there are several arguments that may be put forward in support of it. The first is that the idea orginated in a 1959 article by Professor Ragnar Frisch, a Nobel Laureate in Economics, who prepared a number of computer programmes to show that it was feasible. The second is that a plan of roughly this sort is already in practice in the trade exchanges of the USSR and the East European and other countries which are members of COMECON. It would be possible for a British government and others interested in joining in such a Plan to make a start by linking up with COMECON. If there are hesitations about forging such direct links with Communist planning, these should be assuaged by the very fact of several non-Communist governments taking part as well as Communist authorities. The third answer is closely related; Western Germany already operates a whole range of long-term agreements and contracts for trade exchanges, not only with Eastern Germany but with other East European countries. A fourth answer is that, while some companies will resist, others will see advantages for themselves in such trade promotion, though they will still be suspicious of their new trading partners. A fifth answer is that the UK's nationalised industries, with necessary additions as part of an overall strategy, would provide a major secure resource of supplies for the Government to offer in exchange for what is a rather more secure collateral.

It is, of course, true that the overall value of non-capitalist trade is limited; the Communist Bloc alone provides less than 10% (Table 9) of the world's trade and most of it is in intra-bloc trade; but this reflects blockades and trade restrictions rather than trade potential. More important than the Communist bloc for Britain in a switch from EEC trade would be the developing countries' trade. Although the trade of these countries is still quite small in volume, nearly two thirds of the world's people live within and the potential for growth of trade is great. What holds back this potential from being realised is not the lack of resources of these countries, but their lack of the means to develop those resources and guaranteed markets which would encourage development. Unemployment is not only a feature of the British economy and the economies of the developed countries; it is still more serious in the under-developed countries and in these it is combined with great numbers of people who are under-employed, working only at harvest time, etc. It is among these people that we must establish solidarity and recognise that their problems are the same as ours.

Nearly all developing countries have some form of trade planning as part of central plans for economic development. Their response to the proposal being made here is likely in the first instance to be most enthusiastic. The problem for Britain, and any other developed countries which joined in trade planning with Britain, will be the prices at which goods can be produced with cheap and unorganised labour in the developing countries. The extension of the giant transnational companies' operations into enclaves of development in free trade zones like Hong King, Singapore, Colombo, Manilla, etc. has already provided a challenge to employment in Britain and the USA. The extension of the practice of transnational companies of processing goods in different countries to make use of cheap labour for labour intensive stages of the process, has been spreading far beyond the enclaves listed above to countries like Mexico, Portugal, Yugoslavia, etc.

It would be a necessary element of any Trade Plan to provide for what are now called social clauses. These are designed to ensure that workers in the developing countries are protected against gross exploitation in their wages and conditions, health and safety provision, etc. and are supported in their efforts to secure a share in the social and economic fruits of expanded trade. Proposals for such a social clause have already been made inside a number of international trade organisations like the General Agreement on Tariffs and Trade. Such a clause would do something to ensure that the result of the Trade Plan was not only to underpin Britain's economic development, but to ensure that this was done without it being at the expense of workers in other countries, but rather as part of a joint advance on a common front. It is the unchallenged power of the giant transnational companies that is now not only dividing and conquering working people and governments the world over, but holding back the fulfilment of interests they have in common. The great challenge of our age which an International Trade Plan could be expected to take its part in meeting, is to find instruments that can forge together the interests of working people in all lands.

We must end where we began, then, with the common interests of workers in Britain and working people in developing countries. No plans for the regeneration of Britain's economy can be made without taking into account this worldwide dimension of human solidarity. To do so would be, not only to cut ourselves off from crucial allies in the Third World, but to deny ourselves the opportunity of developing mutually beneficial programmes of economic advance.

What Labour leaders should be doing now, well before the run-up to the next Election, is to start exploring with like-minded Parties and Governments, both in Europe and overseas, the practicalities of establishing a mutually agreed International Plan for Trade Expansion. The more firmly established such planning could be in advance of an election, the more the public could be reassured about the outcome of radical changes in economic policy, and the more rapidly purely negative restrictions on imports and EEC membership could be replaced by positive alternatives. Tony Benn has been ridiculed and traduced for making it clear that any government introducing the measures proposed by Labour Party conferences would have to do four things in first three weeks of office, reintroduce exchange control, impose import controls, give notice of withdrawal from the EEC and remove the powers of the House of Lord to obstruct Commons decisions. Even to get returned to office with such a programme, let along carry it through in the event, the Labour Party will need to have built firm alliances with good friends wherever they are to be found.

Table 1 UK Imports and Exports by Commodity and Volume Increase

Imports and Exports by Commodity as % of Totals

	1970		1975		1980		Imports & Exports Volume Increase 1970–1980 1970=100	
	Imp.	Exp.	Imp.	Exp.	Imp.	Exp.	Imp.	Exp.
TOTAL	100	100	100	100	100	100	144	158
Food, Bev. and Tobacco	22.5	6	18	7	12.5	7	95	200
Basic Mats	15.5	3	9.5	3	8	3	85	179
Fuel	10	2.5	18	4	14	14	56	264
Semi Mfg.	28	34	24	28	27	30	176	147
of which Chemicals	6	10	6	11	6	11	184	204
Finished Mfg.	24	50	25.5	48	36.5	44	300	147
of which Cars	1	4	2	2.5	4	2	588	65
Capital	7	18	8	19	9.5	15	261	132
Non Oil	90	98	82	96	87	87	171	150

Source: *British Business* 25.6.81

Table 2 UK Imports % of UK Home Demand and Exports

	UK Imports % of UK Home Demand and Exports				UK Exports % of UK Mfg, Sales			
	1968	*1975*	*1977*	*1980*	*1968*	*1975*	*1977*	*1980*
TOTAL	12	18	20	20	18	22	25	26
Chemicals	14	17	21	20	20	26	38	39
Metal Mfg.	7	13	20	28	14	12	21	29
Mech. Eng.	14	18	20	21	28	36	43	46
Elec. Eng.	11	21	26	27	18	27	39	38
Vehicles	4	16	24	28	26	23	43	42
Textile	14	19	24	26	16	19	29	34
Clothing & Footwear	11	20	23	26	8	9	18	18
Paper/print	na	na	18	18	5	7	11	11

Source: *Economic Trends*

Table 3 Volumes Index UK Imports and Exports and UK Consumers' Expenditure and Terms of Trade 1970 – 80

	Export Volume (1975=100)	Import Volume (1975=100)	Terms of Trade[1] (1975=100)	UK Consumers' Expenditure Volume
1970	80	77	107	90
1971	85	80	110	93
1972	84.5	90	111	98
1973	96	103	97	103
1974	104	106.5	92	101
1975	100	100	100	100
1976	109	107	100	100
1977	116	113	102	100
1978	118	120	106	106
1979	119	137	108	110
1980	121	131	112	111

Source: *British Business* 25.6.81 and *Economic Trends* April 1981

1. Terms of Trade $= \dfrac{\text{Export Index}}{\text{Imports Index}}$

Table 4   Exports (FOB) and Balance of Trade by Commodities and Export Price Rises 1970-80

| | 1970 | | 1975 | | 1980 | | Export Price Rise % 1980/1970 |
	Exports £m	Balance £m	Exports £m	Balance £m	Exports £m	Balance £m	
Food, Bev. and Tobacco	505	−1341	1388	−2701	3240	−2379	308
Basic Materials	269	− 909	556	−1411	1466	−1947	330
Fuels	210	− 481	827	−3085	6417	− 172	891
Semi-Mfg.	2782	+ 459	5851	+ 496	14143	+1620	355
Finished Mfg.	4100	+2103	9981	+3241	20726	+3876	366
Others	284	+ 135	721	+ 127	1384	+ 179	—
TOTAL	8150	− 34	19330	−3333	47376	+1177	381

Source: *British Business* 25.6.81

Table 5   Annual Movements in Economic Activity (% per year) UK and World 1971–80

| | UK | | | | | World | | |
	GDP _1970 prices_	GDP excl. Oil _1970 prices_	Non-Industrial Output	Exports of Goods (volume)	Retail Prices	Industrial Output _1970 prices_	Exports of Goods _1970 prices_	Commodity Prices
1971	+ 1.5	+ 1.5	+ 0.1	+ 6	+ 9	+ 4	+ 6	+ 6.5
1972	+ 3.0	+ 3.0	+ 2.2	− 0.5	+ 7	+ 6.5	+ 8	+ 9.0
1973	+ 5.8	+ 5.8	+ 7.3	+ 13	+ 9	+ 8	+ 11	+ 50
1974	− 1.7	− 1.7	− 4.0	+ 7	+ 16	+ 1.5	+ 3	+ 83
1975	− 2.0	− 2.0	− 5.0	− 4	+ 24	− 1	− 4	+ 1
1976	+ 2.3	+ 1.8	+ 2.0	+ 10	+ 16	+ 7.5	+ 12	+ 30
1977	+ 2.6	+ 1.6	+ 3.8	+ 8	+ 16	+ 4.5	+ 4	+ 15
1978	+ 3.2	+ 2.5	+ 5.6	+ 2.5	+ 8	+ 3.5	+ 5	− 7
1979	+ 1.7	+ 0.7	+ 2.5	+ 3.5	+ 13	+ 5	+ 6	+ 17
1980	− 2.3	− 3.2	− 6.8	+ 1.7	+ 18	+ 1	+ 1.5	+ 15

Sources: National Institute _Economic Review_ May 1981; UN _Monthly Bulletin of Statistics_ December 1980; _Economic Trends_ April 1981

Table 6   UK Trade with EEC

(a) by Country 1980

Country	UK Balance in Total Trade (£m)	UK Balance in Manufactures (£m)	Total Imports all goods (£000m)	UK Share % of market
W. Germany	−588	−1996	60	8
France	−248	− 429	40	11
Italy	−412	− 380	28	15
Netherlands	+438	+ 182	26	7
Belgium/Lux.	+ 27	− 18	24	9
Denmark	− 71	+ 115	8	12
Eire	+876	+ 804	5	6
TOTAL	+ 23	−1719	291	7

(b) by Commodity 1980 and 1972

| | UK Trade Balance with EEC (£m) | | EEC share in UK Trade | | | |
| | | | Imports | | Exports | |
	1980	1972	1980	1972	1980	1972
Food, Bev., Tobacco	−1409	−562	54	36	51	34
Raw materials	+ 268	+ 28	16	10	55	51
Fuels	+2804	−102	22	24	67	50
Semi-Mfg.	− 592	+132	52	33	42	32
Finished Mfg.	−1127	+107	53	46	38	28
All Mfg.	−1719	+239	53	40	39	24
TOTAL	+ 25	−585	45	35	44	31

Sources: *Overseas Trade Statistics* and UN Monthly *Bulletin of Statistics*

Table 7 Trends in UK Trade, EEC and Rest of the World 1970-1980

	Trade Outside EEC (£m)				Trade with EEC (£m)			
Year	All Exports	Deficit or Surplus	Mfg. Exports	Surplus	All Exports	Surplus or Deficit	Mfg. Exports	Surplus or Deficit
1970	5803	− 73	—	—	2347	+ 39	—	—
1971	6532	+ 381	—	—	2511	− 191	—	—
1972	6602	− 157	5587	+ 2120	2835	− 591	2371	+ 25
1973	7993	−1395	6714	+ 1746	3444	−1191	3209	− 276
1974	10813	−3209	9176	+ 2640	5581	−2042	4318	− 640
1975	13057	− 921	10856	+ 4393	6273	−2412	4982	− 556
1976	16141	−1800	13476	+ 9850	9052	−2127	7176	− 475
1977	19856	− 545	16423	+ 11697	11878	−1733	9172	− 649
1978	21395	+ 674	17292	+ 4264	13675	−2247	10458	−1623
1979	23648	−3497	18292	+ 5424	17039	−2735	12667	−2731
1980	26550	+1177	21110	+ 7215	20826*	+ 25*	13759	−1719

Sources: *British Business* 19.6.81 and Overseas Trade Statistics 25.6.81.

*Note: This is the result in part of very high values of the £ sterling which collapsed in 1981.

Table 8   UK Imports/Exports and Balance of Trade by Area (% of Total and £ million)

	1970			1975			1980		
	Shares of		Surplus or Deficit £m	Shares of		Surplus or Deficit £m	Shares of		Surplus or Deficit £m
	Imp.	Exp.		Imp.	Exp.		Imp.	Exp.	
TOTAL	100	100	− 34	100	100	−3333	100	100	+1177
EEC	27	30	+ 91	37	33	−2507	42	43	+ 709*
Other W. Europe	15	16	+ 35	14	15	− 268	14.5	14	− 71
N. America	21	15	−480	13	12	− 639	15	11	−1659
Other Developed	10	12	+169	8	10	− 17	6.5	6	− 237
Total Developed	73	73	−219	72	70	−3431	78	74.5	−1258
Oil Exporters	9	6	−120	14	12	− 673	8.5	10.5	+ 840
Other Developing Centrally	15	17 }	+281	11.5	15 }	+ 771	11.5	12 }	+1595
Planned Economies	3	4		2.5	3		2	3	

Source: *British Business* 25.6.81

*Note: In 1974 the UK deficit with EEC was £2640m. In neither year does the figure include the UK contribution to the EEC of £600m in 1979 and £800m in 1980.

Table 9 Patterns of World Trade 1880 – 1980

(percentages except for last line of Table A and last 5 lines of Table B)

TABLE A	1880	1913	1937	1953	1967	1977	1980
Industrial Total	71	67	60	65	70	64	64
to Industrial	45	43	35	44	53	46	47
to Oil Producers				3	4	9	8
to other non-Industrial	26	24	25	17	10	6	6
to Communist				1	3	3	3
Non-Industrial Total	29	33	33	26	19	26	27
(of which oil producers)				(8)	(9)	(12)	(15)
to Industrial	25	28	24	19	14	19	18
to Non-Industrial	4	5	9	6	4	6	8
to Communist				1	1	1	1
Communist Total	—	—	7	10	12	10	9
to Industrial	—	—	5	2	2	3	3
to Non-Industrial	—	—	2	1	3	1	1
to Communist	—	—	0	7	7	6	5
TOTAL TRADE	100	100	100	100	100	100	100
in $ billions	13	28	25	82	214	1150	984

TABLE B

Primary Products (PP)							
% of Total Trade	64	64	63	52	36	42	—
Industrial Lands							
% of PP Exports	42	55	36	40	45	38	—
Index of World Trade							
Volume PPs	32	100	118	133	272	425	506
Volume Mfgs.	32	100	92	170	460	1117	1308
Primary Products Prices	121	100	71	230	193	730	1373
Mfg. Prices	103	100	114	212	245	500	734
Terms of Trade							
PP/Manufactures (Mfg.)	107	100	73	110	88	146	187

Notes:

In 1928 World trade totalled $36 billions

In 1937 Communist trade includes all countries which were Communist in 1953.

OPEC exports were 2% of the World total in 1967 and 14% in 1977.

Non-OPEC Non-Industrial exports were 17% of the total in 1967 and 12% in 1977.

Terms of Trade = PPs prices as % of Mfg. prices based on 1913=100.

CHAPTER THREE

Democratic Planning — Afterthought or Starting Point?

Alan Taylor

Introduction

'Oh, and a bit of industrial democracy thrown in' is a recurring theme in recent Labour Party policy statements on economic and industrial policy. Peace, Jobs and Freedom limited its commitment to a vague "progress towards genuine industrial democracy in both public and private sectors"[1] with no attempt to explain how this related to the major economic policies set out in the document. Sometimes the commitment extends to justifying the inclusion of industrial democracy on the basis of making: ". . . our plans flexible, responsive and democratic".[2] A bit of support for worker co-ops, and maybe member representation on the boards of pension funds are also added to the mix, along with, perhaps, support for workers' alternative plans.[3]

These democratic elements are being increasingly listed alongside the major proposals of Labour's alternative economic strategy on the assumption that they can be added to the other policies without significantly changing the shape of the whole package.

It is encouraging to see how far the Labour Party is moving towards accepting the validity of initiatives which arise from below, from working people. However, there does not yet seem to be an awareness that backing these initiatives will build in a conflict with many of the more conventional elements of Labour policy.

Economic policy is still conceived almost exclusively in terms of macro-economic management. The aim is seen to be to stimulate sustained growth in the economy. This cannot simply be combined with support for economic democracy on the assumption that the extension of democracy will lead to greater public support for the policies of a Labour government. Democracy is not that predictable. If democratic demands are unleashed they can be expected to lead to pressure for changes in the original policy. They are likely to lead to pressures for selective growth in particular areas, since the demands will be based on pressure to meet particular needs rather than on a desire for general economic expansion.

Similarly, proposals such as that for quango type development agencies for the English regions, and the intention to "steer jobs directly into the regions"[4] sit uneasily with the talk of greater democracy, and a greater say for workers in running the economy. It seems that, in its major proposals on industrial policy, little has yet been learned from the experience of the last Labour government. The general conclusion of the recent incisive report by four Trades Councils on Labour industrial policy[5] — that industrial policy will be ineffective if it is simply administered by government, and does not involve a real shift in power to working people — has not yet been taken on board.

Pressure from below, and the clearly adverse effects of a lack of economic democracy, have led to proposals for greater economic democracy being added to the list of Labour Party policies. What has not yet arrived is a realisation that support for genuine democracy in industry must mean a profound rethink of policies which are based on increasing state power and extending centralised planning.

It is important that this rethink should take place soon. The combination of attempting to extend central power, and simultaneously offering the prospect of greater economic democracy, is potentially explosive. It could lead to deep conflict between workers and a Labour Government. Alternatively it could lead to disillusionment when people find that the demands they assert through the new channels opened to them come up against resistance from a strengthened central planning machine.

It is therefore important to examine how we can create a successful combination of the economic democracy which is needed to bring people's needs to the fore of economic decision making, with the power of the state which is essential to crack the domination of capital.

Interpretations of the Alternative Economic Strategy

With only Denis Healey and the Trotskyists apparently still opposed to the Alternative Economic Strategy, there appears to be a good basis for Labour Party unity on economic policy. A policy of economic expansion led by increased public expenditure, carried into industry through planning agreements and the use of oil revenues, and protected from stop-go by import controls, does command a very wide consensus of support.

That is excellent, and it should lead to some real unity of purpose when the next Labour government comes to try to put the policies into practice. The first exception, which is still a major area of dispute, concerns incomes policy.

The other major problem lurking behind this wide unity is that different people have different expectations of the Alternative Economic Strategy. On the one hand it is seen as a radical strategy for the transition to socialism which will lead to the mobilisation of people in its support, and which will lead to a real shift in economic power. This view was set out in the recent book produced by the Conference of Socialist Economists.[6]

The other attitude towards the Alternative Economic Strategy is that it is a tool for better macro-economic management. This approach was reflected in a book edited by Blake and Ormerod.[7] Composite resolution 19, passed at the 1980 Labour Party Conference, reflected this view of the Alternative Economic Strategy, even to the extent of including only a brief reference to 'industrial democracy'. David Basnett, moving the resolution, stated that the need was for

"a whole range of pragmatic policies and a determined intervention by government to retrieve a crisis situation".[8]

Composite 30, passed at the same conference, referred by contrast to the need for direct action to resist redundancies, support for workers' co-ops, support for workers' alternative plans, and an expanded economic role for local government.[9] The inclusion of these elements reflects a quite different attitude towards economic policy from the familar emphasis on macro-economic analysis.

Tony Benn, replying to the debates on these resolutions, called for a commitment:

"to self-management as an alternative either to market forces or the hideous bureaucracy, even of some of our nationalised industries . . ."[10]

This comment suggests an approach based on working upwards from helping people to assert their needs. This approach will not necessarily come up with the same answers as an one which assumes that people's needs will be met through better macro-economic management and efficient centralised planning leading to sustained economic growth.

At present the two approaches lead to the same conclusions on a number of important matters. One is the need to restore the economy to health, and the need for import controls to ensure that this can be achieved. A second is the need for expansion to be led by increased public spending so that the maximum number of jobs is created. A third is the need to tackle the major private companies through planning agreements and public ownership.

However, conflicts will soon emerge. Should economic growth continue indefinitely, or will people's needs be met better by a selective approach? This dilemma was reflected in the Blake/Omerod book which stressed the value of directing increased public expenditure more towards capital investment. However, the same book contained chapters which examined the needs in different policy areas. The authors dealing with defence and energy questioned the need for the two largest current programmes of public capital spending — on nuclear power and on nuclear missiles and submarines.[11]

There will be conflicts over the nature of public services. Traditional hierarchically administered, public services have failed to win sufficient public support for the spending on them to be maintained. If we look at public services from the point of view of satisfying people's need, rather than regarding them just as a tool for economic expansion and job creation, then there must be serious questions about the way the services are run if the necessary public support is to be generated. Greater public support for public services is necessary if we want sustained growth in public spending.

On planning agreements and public ownership, there is agreement about their necessity as weapons against private capital. However, if they are regarded as ways of establishing economic democracy, rather than as means of increasing state power, then major questions will arise about the way they should be implemented.

Similar differences will be found in relation to the economic role of local government, the promotion of workers' co-ops, the reform of the financial institutions, the arguments over using government agencies or elected authorities, and the overall structure of democratic planning in Britain.

Above all, if our policies are to be a focus for mobilisation in their support, then there must be things which people can do as part of this mobilisation. We need steps which people can take, and demands they can raise, in their workplaces and communities. If people cannot become involved in preparation for the implementation of our strategy from now on, then it is unlikely that we will generate enough public support for the strategy to be implemented. Nor will we generate enough pressure on the next Labour government to ensure that the strategy is adhered to. Paradoxically, if we want our policies to succeed at the macro level, we will have to build them on people's involvement at a micro level. If our policies are presented as purely as a better form of macro-economic management then it is probable that we will be dragged off course, due to the resistance of capital and the resistance of the state machine. There will be too little countervailing pressure from people with a vested interest in the implementation of our policies to keep us on course.

Needs-based Democracy and Macro-Management — Why the Conflict?

The assumption underlying so much of Labour Party policy in the past was that power should be concentrated in the hands of the central state since the state machine would be able to judge what was needed and to use its enhanced power to push decisions through to implementation. It was assumed that a centralised planning machine, and public corporations, would act in the true interests of the public. This assumption has proved false so often, and people are so alienated from planning processes that they feel unable to influence, that we would be unwise to limit ourselves to this traditional approach.

The Alternative Economic Strategy will be no advance if it is regarded simply as a tool of macro-economic management. It will not then include sufficient scope for ending the role of economic subservience which most people find themselves in. Unless we construct our economic policies around the economic liberation of people, then they are all too likely to simply reinforce their economic powerlessness.

That is what has happened with traditional Labour economic policy. It assumed that the state knew best, and ended up by imposing the interests of the state machine on the population. Centralised planning has turned out to be a system of class domination. The people who operate the planning system have operated it in their own interests — to create and expand bureaucratic empires, to accumulate capital under their control, or to resist outbreaks of democracy such as the Lucas Aerospace Workers' Alternative Plan on the Kirkby and Meriden co-ops.

We have assumed that the state machine will employ complete knowledge of each problem in deciding on solutions, and complete efficiency in implementation. This is about as realistic as assuming that the private market system operates with perfect efficiency in Britain. The reality is that the class which operates the state machine is too imperfectly informed, and too affected by its own self-interest, to come to objective judgements. It is too large, and insufficiently motivated by genuine commitment, to be efficient. Simply placing more power in the hands of the state machine is therefore not likely to lead to the satisfaction of social needs.

There is a dangerous delusion evident among some Labour left-wing politicians that the chief element lacking in previous Labour governments was a sufficient assertion of political will power over the bureaucracy. Too often they seem to see their own personal accession to power as the remedy to this problem. They underestimate the power of the machine to manipulate its political masters. We need a change in the power structure more than we need a change of leadership.

Consequently, if we were to implement economic and industrial policies simply in order to achieve macro-economic objectives — and therefore implement them simply through macro structures such as the state — we would be unlikely to achieve any real erosion of the economic subservience of labour or any real shift in our economy towards meeting people's needs.

That is why it is necessary to begin the construction of our economic and industrial policies with a consideration of social needs, and with the contrustion or bolstering of democratic structures through which these needs can be asserted.

We should have the patience to wait and see what this assertion of needs adds up to, and then use the state to set a framework within which these needs can be met.

Some needs, and some channels for their assertion, are well established. In these cases we can respond quickly. In other cases the needs still require proper articulation, and the channels of expression are not developed. We should work to open up these areas.

"Growth" the Non-solution?

Croslandite revisionism would have us believe that we can restrict ourselves to concentrating on better macro-economic management because economic expansion will lead to more for all and so cut the need for battles over the distribution of wealth. The macro-economic interpretation of the Alternative Economic Strategy follows this same line of thinking.

The political interpretation of the Alternative Economic Strategy is based on the need to win conflicts over distribution if real progress is to be made. It is based on the point established so clearly by Peter Townsend[12] that poverty is more a relative than an absolute condition. Consequently it cannot be eliminated without redistribution.

Redistribution of wealth is unlikely to occur without a redistribution of economic power, since otherwise it will be obstructed by the power of those at the upper end of the scale. The Green Paper on Housing Finance produced by the last Labour government[13] spoke volumes for the inability of the state to impose its will on the 'haves' without a prior transfer of power to the 'have-nots'. Each direction of policy examined in the Green Paper appeared to be blocked by the fear of offending or taking from a substantial group of well-housed people.

Also facing those who see the aim of economic policy to be to manage the economy to produce growth, is the unanswered question about the desirability and feasibility of continued economic growth. Fred Hirsch[14] has demonstrated that continued economic growth will increasingly come up against the inability of social structures to cope with its effects. Continued growth leads to increased competition for those resources which are genuinely finite, such as space, or peace and quiet. Consequently it leads to a continual erosion of the quality of life.

Continued economic growth also leads to increasingly routine and meaningless work, and to a weakening of community structures due to the pressure for greater labour mobility. People's aspirations for work which is of value to society, and for a social structure which encourages their participation, will be increasingly overridden by a strategy which goes for growth for its own sake. We are already suffering from a crisis of alienation from productive work, and a crisis of crumbling community structure. The pursuit of indefinite economic growth can only make these problems worse.

These are the reasons why it is important to begin the construction of our economic and industrial policies from the bottom up. We will then be able to judge how far, and in what directions, the economy should be stimulated to expand. We will be able to operate public services in a way which wins them public support, rather than in a way which alienates even those people who are supposed to benefit. We will be able to explore how to transfer a greater measure of economic power to working people. We will not be able to do these things if we centre our work around macro-economic policies which are based on the assumption that sufficient growth will eliminate other problems.

Policies which work from the bottom up will be harder to implement, and will take longer to have an effect, than macro-economic policies. However, they aim to have a fundamentally different effect, which cannot be achieved through macro-economic management.

The remainder of this chapter therefore, examines a number of channels through which demands for meeting social needs can be raised. It examines how each of these channels can be developed so that demands can be put on government, and so that these channels can then be used as major elements in the restoration of the economy to health. They can be used as the mechanisms through which the economy is rebuilt.

In this way the scale and direction of macro-economic management can be determined from below, and can be used to meet people's needs and to transfer economic power.

The task ahead of us is not simply one of reconstructuring our economy. If the economy were reconstructing our economy. If the economy were reconstructed on a similar basis to the one which has proved so inadequate, then we will find ourselves just as vulnerable to economic problems as we have been in the past. We need to rebuild our economy on a basis of economic democracy because that is the only way to make the economy more secure.

Local Economic Planning

Under the pressure of growing economic problems, and with the backing of the Inner Cities Initiative of the last Labour Government, many local Councils have entered the area of local economic planning. The drift of thinking is now towards providing local government with a set of more specific powers to intervene in the local economy,[15] so that the bridge-head established so far in this field can be consolidated and greatly expanded.

Before we rush down this road, it is important to ask what exactly the impact of Council intervention in this field has been. A recent detailed examination[16] of the performance of one of the Councils which has been most active in economic policies found that it had certainly succeeded in helping establish more jobs in the borough, and that it had helped firms stay in business.

However, it went on to show that this had not led to the local labour force benefiting, since in almost all cases the firms were simply moving from elsewhere, or the new jobs were of a kind which meant they were unlikely to be filled by local people. At its worst, the work of the Council concerned could be described as a means of transferring resources from the population in general to boost the profits of businesses trading in the borough.

We are therefore clearly not in a position where we can simply boost the cash available to Councils, and provide them with more appropriate powers. If we want the work of local Councils to benefit working people, then we will need to take a far more critical look at much of the work done by Councils in this field so far.

The useful work which Councils could do breaks down into four types — support to private firms, direct help to the local labour force, regulatory work, and the use of their own mainstream activities to have an impact on the local economy.

There is no doubt that many small firms need help, and many firms in the inner city need additional resources to improve their premises and working conditions so that they can survive. The problem with local government providing this help is that the immediate effect of the work may be to make firms more efficient by cutting employment, or to transfer resources from the population in general to swell business profits. This work is therefore not easy to reconcile with local government accountability to a purely local electorate which includes many of the local workforce.

However, the work concerned is necessary. It is similar in type to much of regional policy, to the work of the Welsh Development Agency, the Scottish Development Agency and the Development Commission, and to the work of the Small Firms division of the Department of Industry. If we value democratic accountability, it would be a major step forward to consolidate the whole of this work under the control of County and Regional Councils. They cover areas large enough for the benefits of this work to be appreciated, since the purely local effect can sometimes be adverse.

This approach would be far more likely to produce results which benefit working people than the misconceived notion of setting up yet another array of quangos as development agencies for the English regions. We have seen too much evidence of private firms milking government to be happy with regional policies which are operated by bodies which are not accountable to the local labour force and community.

County Councils would need to be given specific duties to make loans and grants to firms, to make premises available, and to support business aid and advice work. County Councils should receive a grant from central government for this work which, like assistance under regional policy, would depend on the scale of local economic problems. Councils in areas with few problems would therefore receive no grant, and would not be involved in this work. This reform would establish the main body of aid to private firms on a basis where the needs of the labour force are likely to be brought to the fore, and through which help is likely to be delivered in a way that is sensitive to local needs.

Direct Council help to the local workforce needs to be delivered on a quite different basis. It needs to be supplied from a source close to, and accountable to, the workforce, and from a source which can deploy its resources with great flexibility. Otherwise it is unlikely that suitable help will be available for voluntary sector training projects, worker take-overs of private firms, workers' co-ops and other community business, employment advice work, trade union resource centres, and the great variety of other projects which are run directly by or for the workforce.

This points to the need for a general duty to be placed on District and Borough Councils to act in the interests of their local labour force, and for them to have the power to raise revenue for this purpose. It would be wrong to straightjacket this work by giving Councils specific powers. Experience so far of schemes which operate within a detailed national framework — such as loans under the Inner Urban Areas Act, or MSC schemes — is that they do not fit the variety of local needs which arise.

Council regulatory work in the employment field could be given a major boost. Much of the work of policing Acts such as the Factories Act, the Health and Safety at Work Act, or the Control of Pollution Act, is carried out by government agencies of questionable effectiveness.

It would be a big step forward to consolidate these, along with bodies like the Alkali Inspectorate, in a new Employment Inspectorate run by District and Borough Councils. Far more weight would be placed behind these efforts to improve working conditions, and to limit the environmental impact of economic activity, if it were carried out by bodies accountable to the local community. This work would be similar to the present Environmental Health function of local government.

The economic role of mainstream local government services has been examined in a recent pamphlet by Michael Ward.[17] It is vital that the next Labour government should restore and extend the powers of direct labour. Councils should be given more freedom to produce for their own needs, and for other public bodies. The purchasing of supplies and services could be used to help bid up working conditions and rates of pay in firms in the area.

These reforms would place major areas of industrial policy under the control of local government. They would mean that help to industry would be delivered through channels which are accountable to the local labour force and the local community. This would lead to pressure for higher spending backed by real democratic support.

It would also mean that the pressure was for spending which benefits labour rather than capital.

Local authorities are already experimenting in economic development work. The demand for more appropriate powers and more adequate finance has already gained considerable momentum. This is one area where it is clear that there will be strong, well thought out pressure on the next Labour government for action.

Workers' Co-ops

There are at present between four and five hundred workers' co-ops in Britain, employing between five and six thousand people. The movement is growing very rapidly. Most of the large number of new small co-ops are in service activities, such as bookselling, wholefoods, or building, or else in the printing and publishing trades. This limited range of activities is the direct result of the limited range of social backgrounds of the people who have set up co-ops. Yet there are enough co-ops in quite different industries to demonstrate that co-ops need not be limited to 'middle class' service activities.

Workers' co-ops in Britain are therefore a small force, but with great potential. The question is how to realise this potential. We would be wise to discount straight away any idea that co-ops represent a magical job creation technique. They depend for their success on the commitment of their members. This needs to be developed and nurtured and it takes time. People cannot be forced to co-operate. Successful co-ops also depend on a change in people's attitudes. A major educational effort will be necessary before co-ops can become widespread in Britain.

It will also be important to be careful about how co-ops are developed. It is quite possible to set up co-ops within a structure which encourages them to operate in a capitalistic way. This would seem to be the aim of the group known as Job Ownership Ltd., who are mainly Liberals. They are concerned that co-ops should aim at efficiency measured in conventional private industry terms, and at the accumulation of capital.

We should be clear that efficiency and the ownership of capital are only means to an end. The end itself is to liberate people from market forces so that co-ops can produce to meet social needs.

We already have a vigorous workers' co-ops movement which is concerned to work towards this end. We should therefore channel help through this workers' co-ops movement. We do not need additional structures or new models of co-operation, since the existing workers' co-ops movement has already shown that it can help to bring about a major expansion in the number of co-ops in a way that contribute towards meeting social needs as well as creating jobs.

The chief focus of the movement is at local level, in a variety of local groups of co-ops and local agencies. These deserve support, principally from local government. They need grants to employ the full-time development workers who can have such a major effect in helping a wider range of people to come forward to start co-ops. Local government will also need to be ready to respond to requests for resources. Co-ops are likely to ask for grants for feasibility studies and other starting expenses, loan capital, premises and access to purchasing officers.

The workers' co-ops movement also has national foci, and it is important that these should become stronger. The Industrial Common Ownership Movement is the main focus. There is also a new productive co-ops section of the Co-operative Union, and a number of other networks such as those linking building collectives or wholefood co-ops.

A Labour Government could use the offer of help to the movement at national level to encourage greater unity. This greater unity is necessary if the workers' co-ops movement is to be effective at national level in supporting local activity, and in acting as a channel for resources to the workers' co-ops.

Two forms of support could be provided, and both are set out in the Labour Party discussion document on workers' co-ops.[18] The first is to re-establish the national Co-operative Development Agency on a basis accountable to the workers' co-ops movement. Established as a quango by the last Labour Government, the CDA has been a deep disappointment. The fact that it has won continued support from the Conservative Government is a reflection on their appreciation that it has tried to take the politics out of workers' co-ops.

The workers' co-ops movement could have used the £1½ million spent on the national CDA to far greater effect — first to support its own promotional work at national level, and second to support local development work in areas where there was no local source of funds available.

Second, co-ops in Britain need their own investment bank. The French workers' co-ops movement has a bank, and the Carter administration set one up in the USA. The experience of ICOF could be used as the basis of establishing such a bank in Britain with Labour Government support.

Effective support for co-op development work, at both national and local levels, would cost about £4 million a year. If the rate of expansion of the workers' co-ops movement were to accelerate considerably beyond its present promising rate, then this would need the help of an investment bank with £20 million a year to invest to begin with, and more as the years passed. Small beer, but well worthwhile.

There is a great deal of work going on at present to build up a stronger workers' co-ops movement. If a stronger and more articulate movement does develop, then the next Labour government will find that it will be an effective lobby for more resources for co-ops. Our task at present is, therefore, to help start more co-ops and to help build these co-ops into an integrated movement.

Savings and the Financial Institutions

A high proportion of the money invested by Britain's powerful array of financial institutions belongs to working people. Their savings are placed in building societies, banks, insurance societies and pension funds for the security which these institutions offer. In return, people give up virtually all say over how the money is invested.

Labour policy on this subject is a mess. As a result we do not have any clear plans to change the timid conservatism which these institutions show in their investment policy. Nor have we worked out ways of preventing them from sabotaging the policies of a Labour Government.

Labour policy is limited to nationalising some banks and insurance companies. There has also been talk of municipalising building societies, and giving members of pension funds more say in running them. None of these policies could be said to have the same breadth of support in the Party as other elements of economic policy. The unions in banking and insurance are opposed to their nationalisation. More importantly, in no case has it been demonstrated how changes in ownership or control will lead on to changes in investment policy. The link is, rather naively, just assumed.

Greater state control over banks is an obvious necessity if a Labour Government is to avoid its policies being undermined by the activities of the City. The new government in France has shown little hesitation in announcing its plans to extend state ownership of the banking system.

However, it is important to go beyond this. We need to show how we will use state ownership of banks to overcome the deep conservatism of British banking practice which is such a drag on productive investment.

We also need to examine the question of community banks. A community bank is the basis of the success of the Mondragon co-ops in Spain, and interest in the subject is increasing in Britain. It is probable that a community bank could not operate under current British banking law since a local depositor-controlled bank would not be allowed to describe itself as a bank. Community banks could make a major contribution towards building more stable economies in many areas which have suffered an outflow of capital and economic decline. There is therefore a strong case for a new Act of Parliament which would provide a framework for the establishment of community banks.

Investments made by life assurance companies and pension funds are made by organisations which have to seek the highest rate of return in order to guarantee the security of their members' pensions. That is why they operate highly exploitive investment policies, favouring property and South Africa as areas for invest-ment.[19] The large size of these institutions also means that they find it hard to invest in smaller companies,[20] and that they follow trends in the stock market in a slavish way, which leads to the trends themselves being exaggerated, to the detriment of sensible invest-ment.[21]

There is no reason for thinking that state control of insurance companies, or member involvement in running pension funds, would make a significant difference. The evidence so far, from the public sector pension funds and from the involvement of trade union representatives as trustees of some funds, is that the concern to secure pensions and insurance policies overrides the impact of any difference of control.[22]

We are dealing here with inherently capitalist institutions which cannot be run in a way that will contribute towards building a more socialist society. They make people acquiesce in their own exploita-tion by tying people's future security to the success of speculative investment.

Our task is, therefore, to establish good enough state pensions and insurance schemes, funded by direct contributions, so that the pension funds and life assurance companies can eventually be eliminated or greatly reduced.

Building societies present a dilemma to the Labour movement. They were founded as democratic mutual aid organisations by working people. They have grown to become remote financial in-stitutions in which the democratic process is manipulated by the controlling oligarchies.

However, there is no strong case for state ownership in this field.

Any attempt at municipalisation would founder because savers would withdraw their deposits faster than the Building Societies could be taken over.

Since the building societies claim to be democratic, there is every reason for a Labour Government to step in to make a reality of their democracy. They should be made to publish a list of their members so that electoral campaigning can take place effectively. They should eventually be made to restrict their activities to one defined part of the country, and to limit their members to a specified maximum. In this way the members would be able to use their building society as a way of tackling their own housing needs and those of their community. The money which building societies currently attract from people seeking a return on their investment, as opposed to the savings of people who are trying to tackle their housing needs, would then be redirected for more productive investment than its present use — which is primarily to encourage the over-consumption of property at the upper end of the market.[23]

In many cases, working people's savings would be better placed in a credit union. These are community based savings and credit co-ops which can help liberate working people from the clutches of hire purchase companies and shady moneylenders. Credit unions are expanding rapidly in Britain now, following the passage of an Act regulating their affairs by the last Labour Government.

These changes in the structure of the financial institutions would remove the current domination of our economy by irresponsible capitalist institutions, and replace them with a combination of state owned and community controlled institutions. The state run banks would be joined by a state investment fund to plough the earnings of North Sea oil into industry. They would face the stimulus of a strong democratic building societies' movement, and growing movements of community banks and credit unions.

This structure would help ensure that our reforms of the financial institutions do not simply end up by bolstering the power of a clumsy and non-socialist state machine. By building up forms of community financial institutions, the reforms would help place a competitive pressure on the state institutions to ensure that investment is used to meet people's real needs.

The action we can take at present will depend on the institutions concerned. With pension funds and insurance societies, we need more research into the effect of their investment, and publicity for the findings. With building societies, we need people to contest board elections in order to raise new issues about the way funds are invested, and to resist the manipulative practices which are used to prevent outbreaks of democracy. We should start credit unions, and prepare a draft bill which would help unions become community banks.

Industrial Democracy, Self-Management and Workers' Control

The proposals of the Bullock Report on industrial democracy, for company boards to be one third shareholder elected, one third worker elected and one third co-oped, were badly received on both sides of industry. This was because the proposals were to impose a corporatist solution on two sides of industry whose interests are often fundamentally opposed.

It is unrealistic to think that fundamental conflicts of interest can be resolved by getting both sides round a table in an atmosphere of goodwill. If we want peace in industry, then we will first have to win the warfare which is the natural consequence of the control of production by the interests of capital.

It is therefore surprising to see such repeated and undefined references in Labour policy statements to the need for industrial democracy. One wonders whether the lesson of the Bullock fiasco — about the unworkability of any 50-50 sharing of power between labour and capital — has really been learned.

That approach is unworkable for two reasons. First, the priority of labour in economic activity — to maximise employment and job satisfaction, and to produce goods and services which meet people's needs — will inevitably come into conflict with the determination of capital to maximise profit and the rate of accumulation of capital.

The history of the Lucas Aerospace Shop Stewards Combine Committee illustrates this conflict. Their attempts to propose constructive, and profitable, alternative products which would have maintained employment, were consistently blocked by management, culminating in the sacking of the Combine convenor, Mike Cooley.

The second problem arises if trade unions do take up posts on company boards. The worry of the union movement has always been that such representatives, lacking the power to change company policy, would either be ineffective or would become distrusted because they would be seen as advocates of management policies to the workforce. This happened with the experiment in industrial democracy in the Post Office, which was subsequently abandoned. It would happen in any scheme which did not give workers majority control.

There are two keys to success in this area. The first is that all proposals should lead to at least majority control by workers — and sometimes to complete control. The second is that a scheme for industrial democracy should only be introduced when the workforce shows that it wants it. Democracy cannot be imposed through legislation. If any attempt were made to impose democratic structures on uninterested workforces, then the whole experiment would soon be discredited by apathy and the possible collapse of the businesses concerned.

Rather than one monolithic system imposed on industry by government, we need to start at the point where workers already are, and make available a series of approaches to extending democracy in industry, each designed to cope with one of the variety of circumstances which exist.

Each approach needs to be triggered by a democratic decision of the workforce that they want to see their company run differently. Each one needs to lead clearly to at least majority control by the workforce, or else to a strengthening of the hand of the unions in their traditional adversary role in collective bargaining. The intermediate, corporatist, approach, of sharing power with capital should not be an available option.

In state owned industries, and re-nationalised industries, we should be looking at self-management rather than worker ownership, since there is no case for transferring the ownership of capital to the workers. The state needs to retain ownership of the capital, either because the industry concerned is vital to the national interest, or because it operates a vital national network, or because the state is a near monopoly purchaser of the industry's products. Therefore, it is right, in these cases, for workers to manage the industries within a framework of state ownership of capital, rather than for the workers to have entirely independent control.[24]

While, to quote the common saying, nationalisation plus Lord Robens does not equal socialism, state ownership plus self-management would get rather closer. We should therefore ask the workers in each state owned industry whether they want to be responsible for managing the industry themselves. If they do, then a structure appropriate to each industry concerned should be worked out with the agreement of the workers, and implemented.

Labour policy on large private corporations, especially multinationals, is for the state to impose planning agreements on them. The details of the agreements would be worked out with management and the unions. In our implementation of Party policy on this subject we may need to distinguish between three types of circumstances, where the workforce will be seeking different levels of involvement.

First, there will be cases where the workforce and unions are not particularly concerned about having a greater say in the way the firm is run. In these cases our objective should be simply to make the company plan its investments in Britain so that greater benefits are achieved for the British economy. Clearly, the participation of the unions in working out the planning agreement would still be sought.

Beyond this, there would be cases where the workforce would want to use the existence of a planning agreement as a way of permanently extending collective bargaining to cover questions of company investment policy. In these cases we should be willing to back up the workforce's attempts to use the planning agreement in this way.

More appropriate union structures will be needed to make effective use of this new power. We should therefore back Shop Steward Combine Committees. The 1980 Labour Party conference agreed that support should be given to the work of Combine Committees. A Labour Government should therefore help provide them with the resources they need for the research an information back-up required to make their work effective.

The third circumstance would be where the workforce would like to own and run the company. In these cases the most effective approach would be for the workforce to establish a collective share fund. For any state help to the firm, and for any re-invested profits of the firm, shares of an equivalent value would be paid into the collective fund. In this way the workers would soon, collectively, become the majority shareholders. A version of this approach is now Social Democrat policy in Sweden and Denmark.[25]

It is also important that we should have mechanisms available for use when workers in medium sized or small firms seek to have their firms run more democratically. The recent discussion pamphlet on workers' co-ops issued by the Labour Party,[26] contained proposals which are relevant here. The proposals have had an encouraging response from people who are faced with closures and a loss of employment due to management incompetence or due to the rationalisation plans of companies. From the number of cases already arising it is quite clear that the next Labour government will have to have a mechanism ready to cope with requests for help from workers who want to take over their firms. The Labour Party proposal is that any group of workers would be able to seek state permission and state cash to help them convert their firm into a co-op. This proposal should be regarded as the first, rather than the last, word on the subject, since it involves some dangers that the co-ops set up would be too dependent on the state to be regarded as genuinely independent co-ops.

To cope with the variety of circumstances which will arise, it will probably be necessary to have several options open to groups of workers who want to take over their firm. In larger firms the option of setting up a workers' collective share fund may be the best, with the workers winning majority control after a few years. In smaller firms with a good enough level of profit to allow the repayment of the owners' capital (or the owner's capital previously bought out by the state), then a normal co-operative can be set up. In firms where a burden of capital repayment would undermine the firm, then it might be better to operate it as a self-managed state or municipally owned firm.

In these ways a variety of routes to self-management and workers' control can be opened up. They are likely to be more effective than the '50 – 50 sharing' style of industrial democracy, since they are far more likely to win the genuine support of the workforce.

We should, of course, guard against schemes which offer workers an apparent degree of democratic control, but which are really designed to co-opt the workers' loyalty to the objectives of capitalism. We should withdraw the incentives brought in to encourage employee shareholding. We should beware of the form of workers' capitalist 'co-op' where workers are required to supply a significant amount of capital to the co-op, and are required to participate in the capital growth of the firm. We should give no support to the latest fashion, which is for management buy-outs in which differential shareholding gives more votes to higher salaried employees and so ensures a continuation of management control.

There is plenty of work which can be done now to prepare for the election of a government which would help with moves towards workers' control. Although it is difficult, we should encourage groups of workers who want to resist redundancy by taking over their firm or factory as a co-op. We should also give support to the development of Combine Committees and workers' alternative plans, since they form an essential part of the raising of consciousness which is necessary if workers' control is to succeed. In particular we should fight to preserve and expand the expert back-up institutions such as CAITS, which is needed to make this work more effective.

The opening up of real routes to industrial democracy will generate pressures on government from workers for greater investment on a basis which will help secure jobs and re-orientate production towards meeting social needs. This is exactly the type of pressure which is needed if our attempts to rebuild the economy are to win the genuine public support indispensable to success.

Making public services more responsive

Our fight back against the cuts is made harder by deep cynicism about public services, even among those people who are supposed to benefit most from them. Council tenants are often deeply hostile to the people who administer their housing, and the feeling is frequently reciprocated. Patients in hospitals commonly feel treated as units on a production line. Users of public transport are often deeply critical of the poor service they get for the high fares charged.

The response of the state machine to this alienation has been to attempt to temper corporatism with 'participation'. Where public participation exercises or structures such as neighbourhood councils have been introduced they have usually been seen eventually as attempts to win support for the existing mode of operation of services. They have not led to real changes in the location of power, or in the way services are run.[27]

The lack of public support for public services, even among those who benefit from them, made it easy for the Conservatives to label public spending as wasteful and a drain on the economy. They won the public argument for cuts in public spending. Until people are really demanding improved public services, it will be hard for us to win public consent for increased public spending.

In order to win this public support we will have to reform our services so that they are run in a way that makes them more open to feedback from their consumers. We should not think that this will be easy to achieve. It will require considerable skill to strike the right balance between public ownership and consumer involvement.

Bringing control of services closer to people, so that they feel able to affect the way in which the services are run, can take a number of different forms. Some of these involve the structure of local and regional government in Britain. Others will involve direct participation by consumers or workers in running the services.

The new French government has started the task of decentralising the French state, so that services administered locally are under local democratic control. It is often not appreciated how far local democracy has been eroded in Britain. Even before Mr Heseltine's assault on its financial independence, local government had lost many functions to regional agencies answerable to central government. New regional agencies had also been set up to administer functions of central government.

As a result we already have regional government in Britain. It is undemocratic, and the different functions are discharged within structures which use different regional boundaries. The water, health, police, gas, electricity, regional planning, manpower planning and employment services, for instance, are operated in this way.

There is a fundamental choice to be made here between two different routes to democratisation. On the one hand, regional government could be established properly, bringing together under one democratic regional structure the functions which are currently discharged by regional agencies and regional offices of Whitehall ministries. To avoid creating too many tiers of government, County Council would need to be scrapped and their functions divided between Districts and the new regions.

The alternative would be to transfer some of the functions of regional agencies — police, manpower planning, training, services to the unemployed, community health, the general practitioner service and, perhaps, hospitals — to County Councils.

The second element of any strategy to make public services more open to the influence of the people who use them would be to transfer functions from Counties (Regions in Scotland) to Districts and Boroughs. It is absurd that County Councils should be cutting (or rather, failing to cut) grass verges on minor roads and helping to choose the colour of paving slabs in new shopping centres — to quote two examples I have come across recently. Social services in particular should be a District function, throughout the country and not just in London, to re-establish the link with the housing service. Some people would go further, and urge the abolition of County Councils, whether or not regional authorities were set up.

The third element concerns correcting the over-emphasis which has been placed on economies of scale in the performance of public services. There are a number of services which could be carried out with greater sensitivity to local needs by parish or neighbourhood councils. Street sweeping, the maintenance of footpaths and smaller public open spaces, and possibly refuse collection, could all be carried out more effectively and with greater support from the public if the management of the local element of the service was open to feedback from local people.

Giving neighbourhood and parish Councils real functions such as these to discharge would help solve the problem of these Councils degenerating into powerless grumble committees which create more disillusion than activity.

Next, there is the question of direct consumer management of public services. Not all public services are suited to consumer management by any means. For the consumers to manage a service effectively, they must be interested in doing so. The service must also be one through which the users naturally meet and so are naturally able to discuss the service together and form common views about it.

The two principal services which fit these criteria are the management of Council housing estates, and the running of primary schools. The establishment of housing management co-ops, and of school governing boards which are more representative of staff and parents, would be likely to lead to both more responsive services and to pressure for higher spending.

Too many other services are administered to people as individuals rather than as groups. Consequently the users are only able to respond in a personal and often selfish way. If we want to see pressure on public services which is based on group social needs, then we will need to run services so that they are delivered to people collectively. In that way people will be able to react to the services collectively, and perhaps run them collectively. Too often, at present, the authorities are able to retain their power over the consumers because the consumers rarely meet.

There are also public services which could be better operated as self-managed enterprises, run by their workers, but owned by the local authority. These are services where the workers are in regular contact with one another, but the users are not, and where the service can be run within clear guide lines laid down by the local authority. Public transport, particularly bus services, are the most obvious example. The quality of London's bus service, for instance, is undermined by worker resistance to its unsuitably hierarchical management.[28]

As in the case of the establishment of real democracy in industry, there is no single monolithic approach in this field. Instead, we need to look at a variety of ways in which public services can be brought closer to people. The effect of this will be twofold. First, there will be effective pressure for the services to be performed in a way that comes closer to satisfying people's needs. Second, this will lead on to real pressure for higher spending because people will value the services more highly. Without this increased support for public spending, our plans to use increased public spending as a way of stimulating the economy back to health will lack the basis of public support which they need if they are to be successful.

Meanwhile, we should do what little is possible when cash is so short to experiment with better ways of running local government services. In my children's school the importance of the supplementary rate increase levied by the ILEA has been brought home to parents because it will help preserve one additional teaching post which has been used to involve parents in the work of the school. This type of direct link between the taxes people pay and the service they receive needs to be rebuilt. Then there will be hope of building real public support for public spending.

Democratic Planning

Working as I do as a local government officer, and having previously worked as a civil servant, I know that the state machine jumps and does what it is told if effective political pressure is applied to it. The problem is one of getting effective pressure applied, rather than one of the immunity of the state machine to pressure.

Left to itself, the state machine prefers consensus policies, since they mean a minimum of change when parties succeed one another in power. Consequently effective political intervention, from outside the government machine and not just from ministers, is vital if the policies of the next Labour government are to be implemented.

Left to itself, the state machine will try to extend its control outwards through structures which are created in its own image. Conventional state corporations, regional boards and quangos fit well with the central macine. Effective local democracy and support for workers' take-overs, for instance, do not. Similarly, we should not delude ourselves that we can achieve our aims through the better management of capitalism. Without structural changes, and a shift in power from capital to labour, the interests of capital will be able to cream off the benefits of better economic management.

Our task, if we want the next Labour government to succeed, must involve the construction of a political process which favours our aims. It is not sufficient to win an election and then seek to implement our policies through existing structures. Unless we change the structures, our work will be frustrated and undermined. There are several types of structural change needed. First, we should limit direct control by the state machine to those areas in which it is really necessary to have undiluted state control. We should not assume that we can trust the state machine to run services in the way their political masters intend. Wherever possible we should establish democratic rather than bureaucratic ways of running public services and the economy, even if this sometimes takes power out of our direct political control. Placing power in the hands of a democratic structure which is accountable to the people we want to help is more likely to lead to or aims being achieved than keeping power in the hands of a bureaucracy which we do not really control. The main areas in which we will need to act to democratise activities which have been colonised by the state machine are the nationalised industries, the army of regional agencies and quangos, and the functions which have been taken away from local government.

Second, we need to be clear that unless we erode the power, and attack the structure, of capitalism, it will in return limit the freedom of action of a Labour Government. In some cases capitalist organisations will need to be brought under state control or democratic control. This is the case with banks, industries denationalised by the Conservatives, and firms which workers want to run themselves — either as co-ops or through the mechanism of a planning agreement.

In some cases we should resist the temptation to try to run inherently capitalist institutions in a better way, since it cannot be done. They will need to be phased out. We should consider whether this is true of pension funding and life assurance.

Third, we will need to identify those areas where democratic structures are small, weak, or absent altogether. In these cases we need to work to build up the structures, making careful use of state help to do so. This is the position with worker co-ops, consumer controlled public services and financial institutions such as building societies, community banks and credit unions.

If we structure our democracy effectively, the state machine should be under such pressure for increased public spending and for intervention to help the labour force achieve its aims, that it should not know where to turn for relief. It should not be able to turn to its political masters, since they should learn the lessons of previous Labour governments and recognise that the intervention of effective political pressure will help them to achieve their aims, even if it often leads to the aims being modified. Too often ministers and governments delude themselves that they can be more powerful by refusing to share power with the Party or anyone else outside. The reality is that this renders them powerless to resist the manipulation of the state machine.

A real expansion of the expression of demands from below for the fulfilment of social priorities will have two effects. The first will be to provide a Labour government with the public support needed to make a success of its politices, and the political pressure which it needs at its back to push its policies through.

The second is to give rise to many pressures for state intervention which were not originally envisaged in the programme on which the government was elected. We should be mature enough to accept that this is a natural consequence of democratic socialism, and to accept that experience and feedback from below will help improve our policies.

Above all, we should avoid creating additional bureaucratic structures — like Development Agencies for the English regions, or a centrally run Planning Commission — which will be presented by the state as bodies which can 'work out what really needs doing, and get it done'. The reality of structures like this is that they operate as ways of imposing the priorities of the state machine on people. Those priorities will not necessarily be the same as the needs of the people we are trying to help. Instead, we should work to build up countervailing pressure from those people and organisations which have a vested interest in meeting the needs of labour and of society in general. If we do not do this we will fail to maintain or generate the public support which will be needed to overcome the forces which will oppose our policies, and consequently we will fail to achieve our aims and so disillusion people yet again.

References

1. *Peace, Jobs and Freedom,* Labour Party, 1980.
2. *Labour's Plan for Expansion,* Labour Party, 1981, Para.19.
3. *Ibid.,* Para.20.
4. *Ibid.,* Para.20.
5. *State Intervention in Industry: A Worker's Inquiry,* Coventry, Liverpool, Newcastle and North Tyneside Trades Councils, 1980.
6. *The Alternative Economic Strategy; A Labour Movement Response to the Crisis.* CSE London Working Group, CSE Books and LCC, 1980.
7. *The Economics of Prosperity,* D. Blake and P. Ormerod, Grant McIntyre, 1980.
8. *Annual Conference Report,* Labour Party, 1980, p.14.
9. *Ibid.,* p.17.
10. *Ibid.,* p.30.
11. D. Blake and P. Ormerod, *op.cit.,* p.104 and p.107.
12. P. Townsend, *Poverty in the United Kingdom; A Survey of Household Resources and Standards of Living,* Penguin Books, 1979.
13. *Housing Green Paper,* June 1977.
14. *The Social Limits of Growth,* Fred Hirsch
15. Review of Local Authority Assistance to Industry and Commerce.

Report of the Joint Group of Officials of Local Authority Associations and Government Departments. Chairman, Wilfred Burns, July 1980. DoE. Also contains a summary of a draft Small Firms Assistance Bill produced by the Association of Metropolitan Authorities

16. *What Local Authorities can Achieve: The London Borough of Hammersmith and Fulham.* P. Motyer and A. Taylor, CES, 1981.
17. *Job Creation by the Council: Local Government and the Struggle for Full Employment,* M. Ward, IWC 1981.
18. *Workers' Co-operatives,* Labour Party, 1980.
19. *Your Money and Your Life,* Counter Information Services, Anti-Report 7.
20. *Pension Funds and the Ownership of Shares of UK Companies.* R. Minns, CES Research Series, 27, 1979.
21. *Finance for Investment,* NEDO, p.115.
22. *Pension Funds.* Green Ban Action Committee, quoting Economist Intelligence Unit.
23. *The Building Societies,* M. Boddy, MacMillan, 1980.
24. *Self-management: Economic Liberation of Man,* J. Vanek, Penguin Education. 1975.
25. *Employee Investment Funds,* R. Meidner, George Allen and Unwin. For a detailed discussion of the application of this approach to Britain see *Democratic Planning Through Workers' Control,* A. Taylor. SERA, 1981.
26. *Workers' Co-operatives,* Labour Party, 1980.
27. *The Local State,* C. Cockburn, Pluto Press, 1977.
28. *In and Against the State,* London Edinburgh Weekend Return Group, 1979.

CHAPTER FOUR

Workers' Plans

Stephen Bodington

The prospects for the UK through the 1980s are: "Absolutely terrible within the framework of existing policies or anything like them . . . As soon as oil stops contributing . . . we shall see something I can only describe in apocalyptic terms". This is the view of Wynne Godley, the Director of the Department of Applied Economics at Cambridge.

Most of us in the Labour movement who have thought about our economic situation would not dispute Wynne Godley's verdict; but were one to ask a randomly chosen person of intelligence whether the Labour movement knows what new "framework of policies" is necessary, the probability is that she or he would say 'No'. That answer is both right and wrong: wrong because there is a seething, fertile, creative understanding coming to birth up and down industry and in the community; right because this creative new activity and thinking has yet to grip the consciousness of the Labour movement as a whole and be firmly built into effective Labour policies that are widely known and accepted, together with the organisational forms capable of implementing them.

Most people don't know how much positive thinking there is about alternative ways of using our resources amongst workers in industry and amongst community activists. From the membership of the trade union and Labour movement there is already beginning to emerge a new economics, pointing a course away from the looming disasters and laying foundations for a thriving, viable democratic society. However, against all the positive new thinking and new organisational developments, there is launched the most violent offensive in defence of the existing power structures. It is only in this light that Thatcherism makes sense: by creating massive redundancies and breaking up whole industries, it shatters the foundations of trade union strength and directly attacks the shop-floor leadership, that is, the shop stewards' movement. This offensive defends capitalist competition and the freedom of capital — now predominantly transnational — to pursue power and profit by whatever means it chooses on the international arena. Such freedom for transnational capital spells loss of freedom for trade unionism and democracy. Public expenditure, on which the economics of social advance depends, is mercilessly attacked.

However, this is not at all the picture that the media give, so, naturally, people are confused and at a loss; the issues that have to be resolved are not clear to them. To blame hostile media for not being helpful is absurd; when we blame the media we are really blaming ourselves. The Labour movement has failed so far to provide itself with adequate means of communicating the information, views and issues that are important for democracy and socialism, indeed, without which democracy and socialism cannot grow. It therefore depends for information on media that support the capitalist offensive. It is as if the body politic of democracy lacked its own nervous system or was fed with messages from outside like a mesmerised patient.

The greatest weakness in Labour's Alternative Economic Strategy is the lack of wide general understanding of it and wide general participation in the making of it. If positive alternatives are to be achieved it is necessary that Labour men and women take into their own hands the tackling of their economic problems. So Labour's alternative must include means of wider involvement in the shaping of Labour's policies and better communication of issues and experiences.

The two pillars that will support Labour's alternative are:
- local and community enterprise using Local Government to faciiate provision for social needs and to create opportunities for people to decide for themselves how this is to be done;
- workers' plans in industry and large-scale undertakings generally so as to use their resources to better social purpose, to prevent redundancies and to prepare new uses for capacity that will be released when the arms race is stopped.

It is to the latter — workers' plans — that this chapter is addressed, but to get to the point of them they need to be seen in the context of Labour policy as a whole and the opposing challenge that defends the framework of competitiveness as an arena for transnational capital. Moreover, it needs to be stressed that wider awareness of what the workers' plan movement is about is essential, not only to the success of these plans in themselves, but also to the viability of any Labour alternative. The driving force and power base of Labour's alternative can only be Labour people themselves and this requires a deeper membership awareness than has been called for in the past. It requires a very firm trade union base on the shop floor in centres of industrial strength.

There are some seventeen groupings of Combine Shop Stewards' Committees that have been working towards workers' plans and meeting from time to time to discuss trade union strategy and organisation in answer to the corporate power of the transnational companies. This is a significant beginning.[1]

Significant as this development is, it is no more than a beginning: the hands that guide British industry are still those that direct some hundred transnational companies and financial institutions.

The workers' plans that have most fired the imagination are those of Lucas Aerospace, Parsons and other firms in power engineering, and Vickers.[2] The detail of these plans is well worth reading; however, workers' plans are more than the plans themselves — much more — and circumstances in different organisations vary greatly. What the workers' plan strategy has in common for different times and places is:

i. it requires involvement and conscious support from the workforce as a whole, blue and white collar workers, all the men and women unified by the fact of working within the same organisation with one common direction, and

ii. it needs to make its starting point a real and deep understanding of the nature and purposes of the organisation as it is at present, understanding of why its activities take the forms they do, what are its dominating objectives, what prospects the future holds.

Understanding the organisation of which one is part is by no means easy, but once workers come together (with perhaps some outside advice on where and how to start), it is surprising how much collective knowledge they find they have. Or rather it is not surprising — for it is they, after all, who make the organisation what it is, make it function. The knowledge that management has is pieced together from knowledge that employees have. It is the piecing together that gives capital the knowledge it wants. The starting point of a workers' plan strategy is the bringing together of their own knowledge for their own purposes. Employees collectively begin to enquire about *the social use of their labour*.

The employees of capital have hitherto been a 'factor of production' co-ordinated by capital and oblivious to the whole of which their labour is a part. Now concern about economic prospects

moves the workforce collectively to pause and look at their employment in a new light; to ask questions that always before had been
left to management, to capital as co-ordinator of economic activity. This is, indeed, a revolutionary step, for almost invariably the
answers to the question "What are the objectives and prospects of
this organisation?" are surprisingly different from what was expected. Experience and knowledge from different individuals and
groups have to be built into a coherent and meaningful whole. And
often this turns out to be very different from declared aims and
prospects. (Again, perhaps not surprisingly after all?). A management representing the interests of capital or centralised state power
may very well have to pursue aims that are far different from those
of their employees.

Consider, for example, a firm that is part of a transnational company pursuing aims dictated to it by the whole framework of
capitalist competition, namely, to make as much money as possible
and to increase commercial strength as widely as possible *on the
whole world arena*. Or consider a Government that is anxious to
help capital to be competitive. Clearly if such are the primary aims
of organisations, they will conflict with employees' concern for
reasonable conditions of work and security of employment. The
supposed and declared aims of organisations will turn out to be
very different from real aims.

The discovery of the real direction in which the organisation is
tending (and how different this may be from the supposed purposes) is the first great step in the workers' plan strategy. This first
step leads very obviously and directly to a second question: "What
is the future that we wish for this organisation? To what useful
ends could its resources be put?"

It is important to recognise the key importance of this understanding of the present, the organisation as it is, its present purposes,
directions of development and so forth. Often workers in Leylands,
British Steel and elsewhere hear admiringly of the Corporate Plan
produced by Lucas Aerospace Combine Shop Stewards' Committee or the contracts won by the power engineering workers to
preserve a British turbine industry, and regret with sighs of resigna-
tion that their own circumstances are so different. It is true, of
course, that their circumstances are vastly different; but almost
every organisation is in a totally different situation from every
other. In terms of brass tacks, the strategies of separate organisations will need always to be totally different; but the starting point
for working out such strategies will have a common inspiration and
a common purpose for almost any of the large scale institutions

that form the framework to the way we live socially and economically. This starting point is to understand the institution, the organisation of which we are part, as it is, the objectives and purposes it is really pursuing, what determines its aims, who takes the decisions that matter, why these decisions and not others, and how decisions are implemented.

Had Leyland and British Steel used the collective wisdom of all their employees to work out *for themselves* where the organisation was heading they could not have failed to be 'better armed against the sea of trouble' — in which they are now drowning. Lucas still have tough battles ahead, and some of their battles they may lose: but they will be greatly strengthened as the number of Combine Shop Stewards' Committees alongside them grow. Then they will be able to look for better use of their resources in conjunction with others, together adding up to a continually expanding section of the industrial resources of Britain as a whole. (The added political strength of mutual support is perhaps the most important thing immediately, but there is also a positive economic significance for the future. Lucas resources, for example, combined with car firm resources, could provide the industrial foundation for a really effective integration of transport systems).

This basic starting point of the Workers' Plan strategy does not only apply to industrial organisations; it applies to any organisation. The starting point for better social use of resources whatever their function — in a hospital, in a university, in a Local Authority office or in a bank — is to understand very realistically what at present makes the organisation tick — or not tick — what its real functions are, how its resources are at present being allocated and co-ordinated. Out of such collective understanding of the present — which the collective wisdom of employees themselves always makes possible — spring automatically criticism and understanding of how resources could better serve social needs. This understanding is the key resource on which Labour's social and economic alternatives have to be founded.

The new situation in Britain which Labour now faces will obviously call for the development of new organisational forms. To group trade unionists primarily by skills and types of work (welders, electricians, engineers and so forth in separate unions) served well enough, maybe, when bargaining over wages — nationally or locally — was the key issue. Today technological change and transnational planning by the dominant firms brings to the fore problems that can only be met by unifying the workforce as a whole at the place of work and bargaining for alternative production plans to safeguard an industrial base for community life. Community interests are rooted in particular geographical environments; the interests of transnational companies are governed by the economics of competition on a world scale. Alternative production plans call for strength and knowledge to set against the corporate power of capital. This implies the fullest conscious understanding and involvement of the workforce as a whole.

The democratic roots of the organisation through which workers are represented have to be patiently and thoroughly developed. This calls for careful discussion and careful working out of acceptable procedures. Setting up and drafting a constitution for the Lucas Aerospace Combine Shop Stewards' Committee took from 1969 to 1974. Where Combine Committees have skimped shop-floor discussion they have proved to be weak in face of attack. The essential guarantee of strength is good communication and full awareness at the grass roots of every move and counter-move between management and the trade union representatives. For example, the difficult struggle at Gardners against redundancies succeeded because for some years previously shop stewards had established the practice of immediately reporting back to those they represented on the shop floor. "Communication", in the words of a Gardners' representative, "is the name of the game." For similar reasons Combine Shop Stewards' Committees are finding it essential to publish Combine newspapers.

Involvement of as many workers as possible in Combine Committee activities draws in a wealth of untapped experience and wisdom and, at the same time, is a sort of 'learning by doing' education in politics. This is clearly demonstrated in the Report *State Intervention in Industry* mentioned above. This enquiry was co-ordinated by the Coventry, Liverpool, Newcastle and N. Tyneside Trades Councils. Some hundreds of workers in touch with the needs and problems of these cities or working with shop stewards' committees in these areas examined their own experiences of Labour's economic policy and performance during the 1974-9 Labour Government. Collective experience within various Labour organisations trying to implement new economic policies was made the subject of critical examination and out of this has come, not some wider learning of truths long known to 'socialist gurus', but discovery of new truths that the shortcomings of socialist policy in practice revealed. At the heart of these new truths lay a more complete understanding of how active, responsible involvement of workers' organisations at the grassroots could monitor and control the carrying out of Labour policies. Involvement educates the individuals involved and they in turn teach the Labour movement outside what they have learned from their successes and failures.

If the Labour movement does not take to heart the lessons to be learned from Combine Committees in industry and grass roots movements around employment plans for Local Authorities, its alternative economic strategy must fail. For this reason the draft Declaration initiated by members of the Joint Forum of Combine Committees is of great importance. "We believe", it states, "that an effective alternative economic strategy must provide the basis for bargaining positions, campaigning demands and a strengthening of our grass roots trade union and community based organisations now, in face of the increasingly aggressive offensive from the Tories and the big corporations alike. A strategy for a future Labour government is not enough. It is all too likely that there will not *be* a future Labour government unless we can win victories now".

In a later section the draft Declaration says, "an effective alternative strategy from a trade union point of view has to start from a rejection of competitive success as the objective of industrial reconstruction. Instead, our proposals must start by linking the social needs still unmet as a result of the run-down of public services with the resources (particularly human resources) of the manufacturing, energy and construction industries. We are not, and cannot be, an isolated economy, so that once our proposals have, as far as possible, linked national needs to national resources, we must then identify the international economies with which we can build trading relations, based again, on mutual needs and resources".

This line of attack is fully complementary to the case made by Michael Barratt Brown for planned foreign trade. An alternative trade policy cannot succeed unless backed by the power of politically conscious, determined labour organisations at the grass roots. Moreover, the existence of Combine Committee organisations is technically essential to planned trade. As Michael Barratt Brown point out, it is "absolutely essential for governments to have inside knowledge of what exactly is being transferred within giant companies when components and equipment move across national boundaries. Only trade union representatives with direct shop floor contacts can provide this, as Tony Benn found during his period of tenure at the Department of Industry".

The draft Declaration looks towards a future that has to be built out of struggle by new organisations extending the older trade union apparatus to meet new problems. Combine Shop Stewards'

Committees come to represent more than a linking of shop stewards' committees; they are creating new centre of gravity, democratising trade union structures and creating spearheads that make feasible the implementation of an alternative economic strategy. They call into use resources — and pre-eminently human resources — to match the social needs of working people. This fight for change cannot await a Labour government. If there is to be an effective Labour government it can only be as a result of struggle for change beginning from now, beginning from the several situations in which people at the grassroots find themselves.

"Workers' Plans", say these union representatives, ". . . directly reflect *our* needs and *our* interests. in order to generate the fight back now, and to lay the right foundations for future policies, we believe trade unionists should be encouraged to develop bargaining activities which don't accept the employer's view of the business, or of what trade unions can and cannot negotiate over. We have a dozen or more examples of this, mainly aimed at saving jobs, dealing with new technology, and meeting real social needs.

"These Workers' Plans clearly show that it is quite possible for trade unionists to develop their own practical ideas about how their company or industry should be run — in their interests and that of their communities. We believe that such Plans should provide the basis for a new type of Industrial Reconstruction and we maintain that the TUC, our unions, the Labour Party and a future Labour government should clearly direct their policies and actions towards the development of such Plans, and of their use as the very basis of industrial policy and strategy."

An Alternative Economic Strategy cannot be implemented without deep popular support; and equally is it true that it must also be generated from the people. It is important, as the draft Declaration stresses, to discuss the ways in which trade union interests can be effectively expressed in an Alternative Economic Strategy and "such discussion must start now and must start on the basis of how we can deal with the present employers' offensive". In this spirit Trade Unions, the TUC and the Labour Party need to draw shop stewards' committee and local Labour organisations into the job of expressing the Alternative Economic Strategy as concrete alternatives worked out by workers themselves, in factories, mines, in the community. In this way the Alternative Economic Strategy can become a rallying point for the Labour Movement. The offensive we face is appallingly dangerous, threatening every aspect of democracy and working class organisation; we can only unify struggle against this attack on the basis of practical, credible alternatives in the shaping of which people themselves have a hand.

The workers' plan strategy illumines in a surprising way a number of problems over which the Labour Movement has long been stumbling — with puzzled awareness of their importance, but with much hesitation about how to tackle them. The daunting on-rush of new technology carries in its flow a whole bunch of such problems. The lives of whole towns and industries are turned upside down in the name of 'technical progress'. Again and again we are told that we must keep abreast of modern science, that we cannot afford not to use the most efficient methods possible, and so on and so forth. And, of course, it is always added that we must see that technology does not harm people. So trade unionists are consulted — but what are they to do? They may point to loss of jobs and negotiate redundancy payments. They may point to unpleasant working conditions and get some modifications. But, basically, the Juggernaut of Technology rolls on, throwing workers out of jobs and utterly transforming the economic geography of the whole country. All this the trade unions seem powerless to stop. Their weakness stems from having nothing to put against competitive success as the overriding objective of industry. So long as this objective remains unchallenged, efficiency is automatically defined as anything that increases power to compete. Even minor improvements in working conditions are rejected if they impede "efficiency" so defined and industries judged "inefficient" by this criterion are allowed to close and swell the tide of "redundancies".

Escape is only possible by asking different questions about the ends which technologies are required to serve. This is precisely what workers' plans do. And by so doing, they at the same time generate an alternative criterion of "efficiency": and efficient technology is one that helps meet workers' needs and the social needs of people. These needs can be determined collectively by workers in industry and people in the community for themselves; organisational instruments for so doing are workers' plans for industry married to community plans for social services, employment and local enterprise.

The mystery and the menace of new technology vanishes as soon as the question "Technology for what?" can be asked and answered. Workers' Plans and Shop Stewards' Committee organisation make it possible to look squarely and concretely at this question. Collective knowledge can be used to throw light on alternative technological possibilities. A precise assessment can be made of how well they serve or do not serve social needs. Looked at from this standpoint clearly, satisfaction from and enjoyment of work itself is a need of working people that comes into the reckoning as well as the usefulness of the products. Full employment, congenial work, scope to develop talents and capabilities, provision for social and material needs are all interlinked aspects in the process of relating technological potential to social needs — which is what the workers' plans strategy is. Without such plans people lack criteria for defining what is an 'efficient' way of organising production and what is a socially valuable technology.

Workers' plans are plans to monitor the social usefulness of production and to set in train realistic, specific proposals to use resources which the market, profit motivated system fails to use. Social use replaces the criteria of competitive effectiveness. This is a big change — a change from market/money economics to the economics of real things, a resources/needs economics that looks at available resources and matches them to social purposes for society as a whole. This approach to economics is also a big change in that it has to be powered democratically from the bottom to the top. The political power that makes it possible is the collective will and the collective knowledge of working people. These are the people on whose skills and efforts the functioning of society is dependant. Control from below now becomes essential since, whenever the automatic criteria of money, costs and profits are not operating the judgement of individuals must decide what is wasteful and what is efficient, in terms of social usefulness.

Production guided by social usefulness is not an altogether new phenomenon. Public expenditure on social services, law courts, education, military purposes is not motivated by profit, at all events not directly, and indeed, wartime planning of the British war economy in 1939 – 45 directed resources to a wide range of social purposes not determined by profitability in money terms. These included much more than munitions and military equipment and extended to civilian supplies such as rationed foods, utility clothing and furniture and so forth. However, it has been a great weakness of the Labour movement that it has not sharply differentiated the economic principles of public expenditure for social purposes from those of a capitalist market economy. Failure to defend social provision as a matter of principle has made the erosion of social gains politically far too easy. It was possible, for example, for charges to be introduced into the Health Service, for the IMF to press home demands for public expenditure cuts and, in general, for the Tories to slash any public services that cannot be paid for out of the profits of capitalist competition.

It may be long before production for social use decisively predominates over market production. Since workers' plans and community plans are achieveable only where there is the political will and conviction at the grass roots to shape them and carry them through, they can only exist where people themselves want them to exist. A Labour Government of the future will have to have national financial, trade and production policies to sustain the overall functioning of society, and this will include expansionary financial policies directed towards market production. However, it would be a dangerous mistake to present Labour's Alternative Economic Strategy as if it were simply an expansionary Keynesian policy breathing life into that economic body which Thatcherism is strangling. As such it can never succeed. Its success will depend upon a *different kind of economics,* taking over deployment of resources that capitalism and market competition fail to use. It will be powered by people at the base. It will use a quite different economic philosophy, quite different criteria to control use of resources. Institutions governed by the criteria and philosophy of market competition — and this is essentially what the NEB, the NEDC and the "Litle Neddies" were — will not help and may well hinder shifts to move the British economy on to an alternative course. If it is not emphasised that Labour's Alternative Economic Strategy involves *economics of a new kind,* a dangerous ambiguity will remain and lack of conviction about the Labour Movement's ability to achieve real social change will erode political support and strength.

Drawing clear distinctions between the two elements of Labour's Alternative Economic Strategy — production for social use powered from the work people and economic policies at government level — should not be interpreted as meaning that Government level policies are unimportant. Government policies are crucial to the effectiveness of workers' plans. Interpreted this way round, Planning Agreements — the "cornerstone" of Labour's 1974-79 industrial policy that proved to be an utterly empty charade — could acquire a meaningful function. Workers' Plans will have to be integrated into the framework of the wider national economy, and, if managements are to undertake to fulfill plans, Governments must undertake to distribute and pay for any products covered by Plans which are not taken up by ordinary market sales. Embodiment of Workers' Plans in Planning Agreements could formally indicate their social acceptance (endorsement by Government as party to the agreement) and also allow them to qualify for all necessary financial backing. Through such agreements there would also be a linking of home production and consumption to foreign trade plans. The area of the economy covered by such agreements would at the same time be a bulwark against inflation. The only meaningful instruments with which to control inflation are (i) exchange controls to avoid 'importing' the outside world's inflation and (ii) using resources to produce goods and controlling prices. (It is money-backed demand unmatched by products that inflates prices).

One need hardly argue whether the implementation of such a strategy will be tough, cause hardship and so forth. The difficulties are not economic; they are political. We have plenty of resources, skills, basic materials or goods to trade for basic materials. The problem is to so organise ourselves as to use these resources. This means doing things in new ways and as long as people doubt the effectiveness of the new ways, there will be resistance to them. Basically, the logic of the Alternative Economic Strategy is to let decisions on how resources are used rest more with people and less with money. But people who now have money, won't like this. Money gives them power which they like, gives them status, control over the media and much else. This concentration of money power, coupled to a much wider fear of change will constitute a formidable battle array. There is bound to be a tough fight — but a necessary fight, so why waste time speculating how tough it may or may not be?

Since the necessary changes involved in an effective Alternative Economic Strategy touch deep roots in the social structure, trade unionists will have to concern themselves more and more with political issues. Their economic interests are so inextricably tangled with political issues. Also, if the centre of gravity of economic change must, as I have argued, be at the workshop primary level, it is essential that political representatives become more accountable and react quickly to democratic pressures. A new democracy and accountability also become essential in the trade unions themselves; otherwise all that the Labour movement has built up over the years — its political and trade union organisations — will be holding back the driving force of the movement at the base, the spearhead of the crucial change towards which the movement has so long been striving. There are many things that have to be done at once, but in a sense, their logic follows in a rather simple way from the basic idea of workers' plans — people understanding where the organisations of which they are elements, are tending and consciously taking steps to see collectively that they change direction so as to serve ends that they themselves believe in and desire.

One such end is peace. It is probable that human societies race against each other to perfect ever more sophisticated technologies of destruction largely because a blind social momentum governs their behaviour. They go on doing what has always been done and fear to be guided by new purposes. Societies with large military apparatuses think they depend upon the military. The military think they depend upon having ever more powerful weapons. The economy provides work for men and women providing weapons and becomes dependent upon arms orders. The inertial momentum of keeping things going in the same direction furthers the arms race and points humanity towards the day when science-based technologies of mutually assured world destruction will actually be used. Workers' Plans have, more concretely than anything else, challenged the technology of arms production and demonstrated alternative ways of using technology. So an economy based on Workers' Plans is also an alternative to what Edward Thompson has called the economics of "exterminism".

References

1. For further information see "Trade Union Strategy in the Face of Corporate Power. The Case for Multi-Union Combine Shop Stewards' Committees" available from Ron Mills, 163 Ulverly Green Road, Olton, Solihull, West Midlands. Much background information about workers' plans and discussions on them in various industries is available from CAITS — Centre for Alternative Industrial and Technological Systems — North East London Polytechnic, Longbridge Road, Dagenham, Essex RM8 2AS.
2. There are summaries of these plans in Part III of *The Right to Useful Work* (Spokesman, 1978) and in *State Intervention in Industry — A Workers' Inquiry* (available from Newcastle Trades Council, 5 Queens Street, Newcastle-upon-Tyne).

CHAPTER FIVE

Job Creation

Mike Cooley

The decision of the new French Government to examine the Lucas workers' Corporate Plan and "other non-capitalist forms of production" is likely to mark a shift in the manner in which the so-called technologically advanced nations view the means of dealing with structural unemployment. Despite the shrillness and aggressiveness of the monetarists (whether in the form of Mrs Thatcher in the United Kingdom or President Reagan in the United States), unemployment, far from going away, is on the increase. Even the massive arms expenditure, which is unacceptable, on a series of other counts, is also failing to curb the rise in unemployment. Predictions of 20 million unemployed by 1988 in the EEC countries alone are no longer regarded as alarmist.

Coupled with this there is a growing recognition of the cost of unemployment in a framework of analysis which was projected early in the '70s when the first workers' plans were being drawn up. This suggests that we shall have to counterpose the micro-efficiency of multinational corporations as they become more and more capital intensive with the macro-inefficiency at the level of the nation state, as it has to bear the cost of growing structural unemployment. In most industrialised nations if a worker with a couple of dependants is unemployed the cost to the state is approximately 100% of the average industry wage, made up by about 55% of transfer payments and 40% to 45% as loss of revenue to the nation state. These are merely the first two economic multipliers. If in addition one takes into account the loss of productive capacity to the nation state and the social multiplier effects such as the degradation, the neuroses, the inter-personal violence, the decline of inner city areas, the illness which is directly related to unemployment, some of which Brenner in the United States has quantified, we begin to get some measure of the cost to the nation state as a whole of the apparent efficiency of market-based capital intensive forms of production. It is said that the riots in Toxteth alone will have cost something in the order of 45 million pounds. This is not a problem peculiar to Britain. The situation in cities like Detroit in the United States has been significantly worse for many years.

It seems clear then that there will have to be some change and this presents both dangers and opportunities. If the Left fails to demonstrate that there are real alternatives which are both non-bureaucratic and non-statist, and which can involve masses of people in developing their own skills, abilities and solutions, then a real danger exists that there will be a polarisation to the Right, and there will grow an attraction, as in Germany in the '30s, to the law and order brigade. The emphasis on equipment for the police and the recent establishment of "camps", are indicators of the way the situation could develop. The other measures proposed by the Government clearly will not work. Mr Heseltine has called in to assist those very people whose economic system has caused the problem in the first instance, and such solutions as they propose are based on the primitive forces of the market linked to capital and energy intensive forms of production.

There is, too, the emphasis on small businesses. The internal dynamic of small businesses is to become big businesses, and each small businessman is encouraged to be an embryonic Arnold Weinstock. Even where sympathetic Labour Councils are able to intervene, there is a tendency to believe that the problem can be solved simply by making public funds available, in a manner which induces passivity and dependence in those communities which receive such assistance. The increasing interest in community work is unlikely to provide a solution either. In many instances it is merely a form of therapeutic activity involving the unemployed in cleaning up and recycling the rubbish which the multinational corporations have produced. These tendencies can lead to a dual economy. On the one hand a tiny minority will work for the vast multinational corporations and as a result enjoy international travel, company cars, medi-care and a comparatively high standard of living. On the other hand, the increasing numbers displaced by these policies may be driven back into "community activity" where they will have no economic or political power in the traditional sense of the word. Meanwhile, the multinationals will dominate the manner in which science and technology develops and is applied, and will even determine the educational framework in which new technology is to be introduced. This will give rise to a new form of "feudalism".

useful production provide one part of a real alternative policy. These plans regard human skill, ability and enthusiasm as assets, something which human society should treasure, encourage and enhance. These plans also provide a framework in which human beings can play in a complementary way their dual role in society, as both producers and consumers. This could provide the basis for overcoming that situation in which producer is counterposed against consumer, in which human beings are required as producers to perform grotesquely alienated and fragmented tasks in order to mass-produce rubbishy throw-away products; whilst the same products provide the basis for exploiting human beings as consumers. These workers' plans would change dramatically our concept of what actually is a "viable product". If, for example, we use the monies presently paid as unemployment benefit and produced products which simply broke even, society would still end up with an artefact or a service which would fulfill a human requirement as an alternative to tolerating the suffering of unemployment.

This view is, of course, full of commonsense, yet as far as the market economy is concerned it is perverse and subversive. It is so because it would mean that we began to assess products for their use value rather than their exchange value. Our concept of how products are designed and built could dramatically change. We could design products which would last very much longer, would conserve energy and materials and be produced by non-alienated means. I have described some of these in my book *Architect or Bee*.[1] Strangely enough, confirmation of some of these product ideas came recently from a report by the Battelle Institute in Geneva entitled *On the Potential of Substituting Manpower for Energy*. It pointed out that if car engines were designed to last between 14 and 20 years, not only could we conserve energy and materials, but we could actually provide 65% more work in building products of this kind and repairing them than we do in mass producing them. It will be evident also that the 65% extra work would be diagnostic maintenance repair type work which human beings normally like doing.

So when we are talking about job creation and more work we are not talking about the grotesque, back-breaking, alienating tasks of the past, but work which would link hand and brain in a meaningful creative process, and help to liberate human beings in a political, social and material sense at the same time. These workers' plans have also the great advantage that they would help to link industrial workers with community groups, ecologists, environmentalists and many others concerned about the way in which our society is developing. Further, by proposing equipment for the disabled, for the medical services and for the elderly, they will correctly show the trade union movement how to be what it should be, a caring non-hierarchal, active and imaginative countervailing force to the vast multinational corporations. To begin to do these things we will have to have the courage to question and challenge the given economic categories, as the Lucas workers have done.

We must refuse to allow our commonsense to be bludgeoned into silence by the clap-trap of economists and accountants. In each industrialised nation they tell their own working class that they must have a balance of payments surplus. This is clearly impossible since a balance of payments surplus in one country must by definition mean a balance of payments deficit in another. It is therefore, an extremely imperialistic form of concept. They also point out that we have to compete with other nations. Here they do not, of course, mean that we should compete in terms of cultural attributes or concern for the weak, or in the elegance of our solutions to unemployment, or in programmes for conversion to socially useful work as distinct from armaments and destruction: rather they mean compete in the narrow economic sense of the market. They would hold up to us model nations. The model used at one stage to be Sweden. Then it was West Germany. Then I noticed on a recent visit to West Germany that the German employers say to their workers that they must cease to be greedy and lazy and must be like the Japanese. So the Japanese have now become the international model for us. And as the frantic spiral of international competition removes the Japanese to a second rate place it may be the South Koreans, or some other nation, as has already happened in the shipbuilding industry.

We have by contrast to assert that we want to see our economy and our productive capacity geared to meet the internal needs of the mass of people in this country and also to relate to other nations in a mutually non-exploitable and supportive fashion. This will require the working class in each nation to attempt to shift its own economy in this direction and then make links with workers in other countries, to ensure that relations at an international level assist workers in each country rather than counterpose them, one against another. We will also have to cease to take economists too seriously. It is revealing sometimes to look at what they say. They predict with apparent absolute certainty, and to many decimal places, the rate at which something will go up. If a thing goes down they are quite unembarrassed by this and extremely urbane and point out that it might have had something to do with the price of

oil in the Middle East. If those of us who work in the aircraft industry predicted something will go up and it comes down, then we
are enormously embarrassed by that, because there is physical
evidence that we have got it wrong.

We are dealing with more exact sciences and in a more constrained environment. Economists would like to have us believe that they
are also dealing with exact sciences. Then there is the glorification
by economists and accountants of paper money. Well, you can't
eat a pound note. You can't ride around in it. You can't live in it.
Paper money only has a significance if we produce real wealth
which is its equivalent. And if all those who produce and handle
paper money disappeared tomorrow we would still have miners
mining coal; bricklayers building houses; bakers baking bread, and
engineers designing and producing machinery. This is the great
power that we have and we should never forget it. As we put forward these ideas in the Labour and trade union movement it will be
said that now is not the time to raise them, that the important thing
is unity. But unity of the graveyard is useless. And it would be quite
pointless being united and returning a Labour Government which
did to us again what the last one did.

Workers in industry will still recall vividly the visits to that great
Bermuda Triangle of British politics, the Department of Industry.
In particular they will recall the despicable way they were treated by
people like Gerald Kaufmann and Eric Varley. As Ernie Scarbrow
of the Lucas Aerospace Committee put it, "Kaufman sat there
sneering at us when Blythe threatened to close down the whole of
Lucas Aerospace in the United Kingdom if we continued to press
for our plan for socially useful production". Yet Kaufman had
been committed by Labour Party Conference to nationalise Lucas
Aerospace if the company refused to take up the Lucas workers'
plan. So these questions are related to the issues of Labour Party
democracy, the accountability of Labour leaders and the need to
carry out Conference policies. As the massive problems throughout
the world now confront us, it is clear that the given economic
categories are incapable of providing solutions. We need to be
courageous and imaginative. It is remarkable that there has been so
much technological and scientific invention over the last two hundred years and so little social and political invention.

Clearly we need once again to re-awaken in the Labour and trade
union movement the socialist "dream": a vision of what the future
might be like, something to aspire to. And as we do that, we should
not do it in any utopian fashion, but by demonstrating concrete examples of what we mean. Products on the one hand, like the road-

rail bus in the workers' corporate plan, or the heat pumps which would conserve energy and materials. But also convey the sense of excitement, enjoyment and sheer enthusiasm that the workers experienced in drawing up those plans and making those products, as they gave full scope to their own creativity and ability. I am frequently asked if I believe that ordinary people will be capable of dealing with these great problems. I have never myself met an ordinary person. All of those I meet are extraordinary. They are fitters, nurses, teachers, and all of them bring a vast range of experienced knowledge and ability to the tasks they undertake. And all that ability could be liberated in making this society a decent and a fulfilling place in which to live.

Above all else, we must not accept that the future is already predetermined for us. The future is not out there in the sense in which America was out there before Columbus went to discover it; the future doesn't have predetermined shapes and forms and contours. The future has yet got to be built by people like us and we do have real choices, if we have the courage to stand up and assert them.

CHAPTER SIX

Developments in Combine Organisations

Mike George

THE EMPLOYER'S OFFENSIVE

Amongst many (if not most) of Britain's larger companies, there is a new, politically minded, offensive being waged by employers — British Leyland is only the most obvious example. A couple of years ago the head of STC (part of ITT) called upon employers to mount a *political* offensive in order to curb the power of trade unions. This call has been heeded, for instance over the past 18 months there have been a number of high-level conferences of employers' representatives, all debating ways and means of reversing the supposed growth of union power. A recent conference made it clear that employers expect to have another 18 months or so in which to carry this out.

Obviously the existence of a Conservative Government more radically committed to a free market economy than any since World War II is a very major factor in this offensive. The Tories' adherence to major policy decisions means in practice much more than so-called monetarist policies. Monetarism provides a useful popularist approach to the economy — putting it into the realm of 'good housekeeping'. It also provides one of the mechanisms for putting the economy into a political framework which denies power to organisations in society which do not represent finance capital.

This *political* reconstruction of the nature of the economy means that industrial capital — those that control industry must 'shape up' into a more political force which owes long-term allegiance to finance capital. So, we've seen the CBI upset over the continuation of high interest rates, the over-valued £, and over the 'market' pricing policy of energy. None of these factors directly aids industry, quite the reverse — adding to industrial companies' oft-quoted difficulties in the current trading receccion. Yet many top industrialists declined to support the CBI's position, some even leaving the CBI altogether. Why is this?

It is clear that the Stock Market and other financial institutions have not suffered the decline in confidence which appeared in the mid-1970s; indeed the Stock Market in general is 'bullish'. Finance capital, it is presumed, will be aided by Tory policies.

It would be wrong however, to assume that it's only a matter of the industrialists "having to shape up", for there is more than just a coincidence of interests between Tories and Big Business. Business leaders like Edwardes of BL, Scott of Lucas and Campbell Fraser of Dunlop have operated on the trade unions in a coherent, political way themselves. Trading difficulties are used by them to create quite comprehensive strategies in relation to labour and the unions. For instance it was *no coincidence* that Derek Robinson was dumped, the combine shop stewards' committee undermined, that new working methods were introduced at Longbridge, and that the Mini Metro's 'success or failure' was held up as a symbol of Britain's success as an industrial power. At Dunlop the latest redundancy threat (to 1,800 jobs) was directly used as a lever to try to reduce the power of shop stewards at a number of plant.

The Tories' philosophy also means a withdrawal of support from various parts of society, including unemployed, sick and disabled people, and urban areas suffering from economic and social deprivation. And no longer is the State employer of last resort, it is one of the toughest employers around now. Obviously not all of these features are completely new (the last Labour Government operated monetarist policies), but the clarity of political will certainly is.

While a change in the 'terrain' upon which Government aid is given to industry remains the main direction of policy, albeit tempered by certain tactical necessities, this is being achieved in a way which harmonises well with the Tories' interventions in another part of industry. Conditions are being created whereby one major organised sector of society is being made marginal — because it has historically held a very different view of society and industry, namely the trade union movement. Some of these conditions are being created through direct legislative attacks, such as the 1980 Employment Act, but others are brought about indirectly. The Tories are removing trade union power via the employers. The odd, politically expedient gesture of support for small businesses, or the maintenance of certain regional incentives cannot be read as a 'U Turn'. The post-war forms of political involvement allowed to trade unions, albeit to achieve consensus, are being swept away.

Those employers who understand the longer term aims of the

current Tory philosophy and politics can therefore find a happy coincidence of interests! The recessionary trading conditions, the overvalued £, high interest rates are combining to create the need for companies to radically restructure and slim-down their businesses. This is releasing money internally, which is needed to cover overheads (as production levels are cut), and for investment in labour-saving and other new technologies. The 'internal' conditions created by restructuring, rationalisation and redundancy are, of course, detrimental to trade union power, but many employers are taking advantage of these conditions to directly attack shop floor trade unionism as well.

So the trade unions are facing a many-sided attack. Legislation is curbing many trade union activities, such as secondary action and picketing. Job losses, short-time working and closure threats are undermining militancy and affecting bargaining activities. And there is a continuing ideological attack on unions, through the media and elsewhere, which attempts to portray unions as irresponsible and destructive at worst, irrelevant or useless at best.

The sheer size of the labour shake-out in industry has surprised the Tories, but pleasantly, we must presume. The Government has had to put millions of pounds more into the redundancy payments fund to avoid it going bankrupt. These shake-outs are on a much bigger scale than in the mid-1970s — when companies' liquidity problems were greater than they are now. Reductions in labour have commonly occurred "across the board", affecting many plants (sometimes via complete closure), and often taking the form of enforced redundancies. The effects of this scale of job losses was reflected in the strike statistics for 1980 (the lowest for decades). Trade unions have 'had to' relinquish many shop steward and other union rights and practices. And as the unions have backed down in the face of job losses, so have many employers taken the opportunity of 'explaining' to employees why they must make sacrifices for the good of the company (and for themselves, of course) — often by-passing union channels altogether by writing direct to employees or producing special 'employee reports' on the business.

The companies' lectures on 'business realism' have, of course, been directed towards wages too, the downwards pressure on wages has been aided by threats to jobs — wage cuts or even bigger job cuts. Companies have been only too anxious to explain their view of economics to their employees during this recession. This has been markedly successful in certain sectors such as engineering and a lot of manufacturing industry. Trade unions have been told that there will be no wage negotiations — for the first time in decades some unions have had to forfeit their collective bargaining rights and functions! Wage awards which go nowhere to meeting cost of living increases have effectively undermined unions' major contribution to the membership — the longer term consequences of this are grim.

Changes in the work environment and in working methods, often via the introduction of new technology, are being pushed through on the back of job cuts and the 'necessary' reduction of labour costs. The most obvious example of this is, of course, the Longbridge plant of BL — this being used politically as a symbol of the 'new economic realism', and it's no wonder that BL 'welcomes' Nissan to Britain, for it hopes it will bring into the country's car industry yet more changes in work methods. Hand in hand with these new methods is an attack on shop stewards' control, rights and organisation (BL, Ford, Dunlop etc.).

So trade union organisation is being hit by redundancy and closure threats, short-time working and the breakdown of conventional bargaining rights and practices over wages and conditions. Shop floor organisation is in great danger, both directly through curbs on shop stewards, and indirectly through the narrowing of areas of negotiation. This is reflected at all levels in unions, right to the level of the TUC.

In general terms there has been only one major change in the areas of intervention and activity allowed to trade unions over the past half century. Bargaining and related activities over wages and certain conditions relating to employment contracts was joined by participation in indicative planning of certain industries. This occurred in World War II, and has continued (at different levels of involvement and activity) up to the end of the 1970s. Bargaining is under attack, and now, despite the continued existence of the Neddies etc., unions' involvement in industrial and economic planning is also at an end — except in the most formal sense. The trade union movement and the labour it represents is being effectively displaced — in economic and political terms. Large areas of economic (and social) life are becoming non-negotiable. If the Tories have their way, trade unions are to become like most other voluntary bodies in society. They will be allowed to exist subject to 'normal' contract and property law, and their sole function will be to provide a certain coherence to what might otherwise be a somewhat too anarchic style of employment and wage regulation.

A Response to the Offensive?

Many people in the trade union and labour movement seem surprised at the lack of militancy amongst those large groups of organised workers who have faced massive job losses, closures, and attacks on trade union organisation and activities. The lack of a believable alternative to fight for must figure largely in this, for without a clear aim the trade union and labour movement has few effective weapons to fight the many-sided employers' offensive.

"But", some would argue, "we've got an alternative, it's the Alternative Economic Strategy". In some ways it certainly *is* an alternative, for it proposes that we spend our way out of the recession through a £6bn increase in public spending, and it's presumed that some of the jobs will come back — directly in the public sector, and indirectly through increased spending, and therefore home demand for goods. It tackles the imports 'problem' by calling for planned trade. It demands that some exchange control measures be introduced in order that capital outflows from the UK can be curbed. It proposes new Planning Agreements in companies, which will integrate into national economic planning. It raises again the use of price controls.

But it also demands more Government aid to industry, and a lot more money to be put into job creation type schemes for the unemployed. It proposes a new National Investment bank to back up a reconstituted National Enterprise Board.

There are many detailed arguments around each of the points in the Alternative Economic Strategy and there's not space here to explore them. However, there are a few matters which should be considered which are, in the end, crucial to the question of whether this really *is* a viable alternative.

Firstly, it doesn't mention anything about *how* these measures are to be effected, and that's because it's assumed that it's simply a matter of having a Left Labour Government in power. This assumption was made in 1973 and 1974, and look what happened: all the rhetoric remained, but none of the measures were carried out, except in the most formal 'top-down' manner. All the Civil Service power, all the *managerial* Neddie-type bodies were unchanged — Planning Agreements foundered and the NEB became a merchant bank. The fact that certain trade union leaders served on the many planning and other industry bodies made not one jot of difference; the bodies themselves worked on the basis of the employers' interests, and trade unionists were nearly always in the minority on these bodies anyway.

It's no accident that there's nothing in the Alternative Economic Strategy about this. For if you look at it closely it is firmly based on the assumption that workers can *only* pursue their interests within an expanding and productive private company sector. The only claim made on the employers' power is that they sit around tables discussing with trade unionists and Government representatives ways and means of increasing efficiency and competitiveness. The Planning Agreements, planned trade and exchange control measures will be applied *within* this framework of business efficiency, for, despite various statements about trade union involvement at national and shop floor level, there is no clear statement about any possible conflict of interests. If you will recall, exactly the same sort of vague commitment to democracy in Planning Agreements was evident in Labour's 1974 programme.

On this basis the Alternative Economic Strategy looks very much like a straightforward return to Labour's Industrial Strategy as pursued in 1974-1979, and we all known that did nothing to aid the 'irreversible shift' of power to working people. In that time company taxation became a joke, with all major manufacturing companies being relieved of the duty to pay tax (in effect), and companies got £10 millions a week of public money through the Industry Acts — with little or no discernible benefit to workers. There's nothing said about tax now, and the proposal is to give yet more public money to companies with no trade union or public accountability over its use (which in many instances is supposed to create jobs).

It has been said that the last Labour Government's Alternative Economic Strategy (the basis of the present one) had the political advantage that it commanded popular support (right up to the day of the election!). But is this so? Over 20 trade union organisations directly affected by the Strategy, and representing perhaps 100,000 or so workers have recently collaborated on a book* which condemns Labour's strategy — and this is only the tip of the iceberg. Another way of looking at this 'popular support' is that it formed the cement of the Social Contract, and bought a few years' consensus between Government and trade union leaderships. Few would deny that a certain degree of consensus might at times be necessary or useful, but that consensus was then, and is now, based upon a managerialist view of industry and the economy in which workers' only involvement is in the form of 'lobby fodder'.

What is also very evident is the fact that the Alternative Economic Strategy ignores the employers' current offensive. It provides nothing for today's struggle, just a set of outline policies for the future, and the political struggle is actually an 'internal' one in

---

*State Intervestion Industry: A Workers' Enquiry. Coventry, Liverpool, Newcastle and N. Tyneside Trades Council.

the Labour Party and certain unions over the precise form of these policies, not actually a political struggle against the forces and agents of the current offensive against the trade union and labour movement. This is not to deny the need for political struggle within the organisations of the labour movement, but it *is* crucial to recognise that this form of politics has done nothing to reverse the erosion of trade union and labour rights. If the employers' offensive is not checked and reversed the operation of the Alternative Economic Strategy will occur in a situation where workers and their representatives have been thoroughly beaten down — this would hardly be a situation which would ensure that the Strategy is operated in the interests of workers (surely history has taught us that!).

This brief and, some might think, rather brutal attack on the Alternative Economic Strategy, is not designed to destroy its credibility completely, for certain elements, like increased public spending would have to be defended. It should, however, help to show that it is not *the* alternative to fire and mobilise the trade union and labour movement against the current policies and practices (Government and employers) and for a real alternative to unemployement and the rest. Some of its 'empty boxes' don't look too bad, but what goes into them must unequivocally be *our* proposals and demands, not the country's managerial elite.

Workers' Plans

The current employers' offensive should be looked at squarely, for the trade union and labour movement has much to learn from it, and not to do this simply engenders defeatism and a lack of informed industrial and political action. How the fight against the employers' offensive is mounted *now* could have profound implications for future industrial and economic strategies.

Workers' Plans are not simply about socially useful products, they represent workforce and community initiatives which are truly *independent* of the managerialist framework of industrial and economic decision-making and analysis.

They are about (i) seeking appropriate and effective forms of union organisations to deal with vastly changed corporate structures, (ii) using knowledge and information obtained through the labour process for getting a handle on those corporate decisions which affect jobs and other employment matters, (iii) using this knowledge and information to build up an *independent* bargaining position based firmly on the workers' view of what they require from the enterprise, (iv) extending the boundaries of collective bargaining and related activities, not accepting managements' definitions of what is or is not negotiable, (v) overcoming traditional divisions between industrial, economic and social policy, partly through production proposals to meet social needs in communities, partly through demands on company taxation, Government grants and the rest.

These plans have in practice represented effective counters to corporate power, mainly by cutting through the fabric of the employers' arguments about 'necessary' sacrifices for the good of the company. There are a number of examples available, covering wages, new technology, job losses and pensions.

In Lucas some 2,000 jobs were saved in this way. The introduction of new technology is being carried out very much under the Combine Committee's terms, these terms are largely embodied in a New Technology Alternative Plan, and a subsequent Model Agreement. Meanwhile, work is in hand to prepare a wages claim which analyses the company's 'ability to pay'; with so many companies formally declaring poor results it's doubly important to look closely at their Accounts — Lucas last half-year results showed an apparent profits drop of over 40%, but the real drop was only some 10%.

In Metal Box, the Combine Shop Stewards' Committee is similarly considering a 'Value-Added' wage claim, which takes little account of 'declared' profit, and looks instead at the rate of extraction of value from each employee. The Committee has also engaged in a number of advance planning procedures, in which 'getting a handle' on the company's intentions and policies has been crucial in various redundancy and closure situations.

In Dunlop the Combine Committee is preparing a workers' plan response to a current redundancy situation, and has started on a longer term development of shop floor bargaining strategies in relation to new technology — especially in tyre manufacture.

There are many other examples that could be quoted, which makes it clear that a growing number of shop stewards' committees do not see their members' salvation in some new version of the NEB — it couldn't help *now* and it won't help in the future. And this view is shared by a growing number of Trades Councils and other local bodies (including some local Councils) which need solutions *now*.

The Trades Councils are trying to join up to present a unified view on industrial policy, a view which is based firmly on the experiences of a great many shop stewards' organisations in their various areas. Similarly, the Joint Forum of Combine Committees (involving some 15 Combines) is bending its collective mind to the need for rank and file based initiatives.

It is not longer true to say that Alternative Plans or Workers' Plans are isolated 'events', although four or five years ago this would have been true. Experience of Labour's Industrial Strategy, and now experience of the Tories and of the employers' offensive is changing the situation to a point where there is emerging a coherent and substantial trade union based alternative — both to current economic and political policies, and to the so-called Alternative Economic Strategy.

This alternative is based on:

  i. The development of new organisational forms, which are more effective in relation to the structures of large enterprises.
 ii. A new approach to getting and using company information, which avoids the 'Catch 22' of normal Information Disclosure provisions — "how do you know what information you need if you haven't got any anyway?"
iii. The development of community-based social and economic audits, which make clear the concrete effects of corporate policies and actions.
iv. The development of Plans for running enterprises in different ways, which are based on the assumption that they should be run for those who work in them and for those in the community that are affected by them.

This alternative can provide effective trade union and labour movement policy and action *now* against the employers' offensive, but it also lays the basis for a much more radical and far-reaching 'alternative economic strategy'. It doesn't make the assumption that workers' interests can *only* be met via a conventionally profitable and competitive private sector, it doesn't assume that the State will provide all, via its tie-up with big business. Rather, it assumes that future industrial policy or strategy should be based squarely on the interests and the intiatives of those who are most directly affected by those policies and strategies — workforces and their communities.

What is being said is that working people *are* quite capable of determining industrial policy, and by implication other policies, such as those relating to the operation of nationalised industries, public corporations, the NHS etc. It is the workers' plan type of educational and politicising experience which will make this real, not forgetting the crucial point that mobilising *now* against the offensive stops all this from being 'airy fairy'.

A new political territory is being opened up — as a result of the frustration and anger of a great many people over what they see as a tired re-run of limited and limiting policy options. They don't want to be offered those nice-sounding but *empty* policies again, they want to put into them policies and strategies which are more than a sell-out. But, of course, much will depend upon who in the labour and trade union movement will see this energy and initiative as a threat . . .

Chapter Seven

Local Enterprise

Michael Barratt Brown

I take it as given that socialists cannot expect to think clearly about a radical transformation of capitalist economic structures, unless they have, not only a clear model of the working of capitalist political economy, but also some model of a socialist political economy. This must be especially important if thinking is directed to the forms of struggle and the alternative strategies which could be developed, both to defend the gains which have been made up till now by working people inside capitalist structures and to generate the political will to advance towards making a radical change in those structures. Unfortunately, while we have a fairly clearly defined model of capitalist economic structures, alternative socialist models are either extremely vague or quite unacceptable to those whose definition of socialism implies the exercise of popular power in the production and allocation of resources to meet social needs.

We have, in other words, economic models of a simple market economy bringing together millions of separate producers and consumers and of a market economy dominated by the capital accumulation of giant transnational companies in opportunistic alliance with powerful state organisations. We have a model also of a command economy based on state ownership of the main productive resources with some minimum delegation of powers to enterprises and localities and with the market exercising the residual function of a commodity economy — the concealment of the actual value added by labour behind the veil of money wages and prices. We have had some attempts to make that veiled process clear through "open books" and publicly advertised shadow pricing such as were made by Professor Ota Sik in Czechoslovakia in 1968 and by the Allende Government in Chile in 1972. What we do not have is a model that links workers' self-management, popular power in determining social needs and the co-ordinating function of central planning.

This lack is reflected in the weakness in socialist thinking about transitional change. There is, in particular, a lack of connection between the workers' plans of combine committees like Lucas Aerospace and Vickers, the employment initiatives of local authorities associated with local development groups as in London, Sheffield, Coventry, Newcastle and elsewhere and the alternative macro-economic strategy of the Labour Party and TUC. Excellent contacts have been established now between Combine Committees and local development groups through Trades Councils and the network of Labour and Community Research and Resource Centres. But the link between the productive capacity of industrial workers and the determination of social needs by community associations implies an economic model of socialist planning that is missing. The alternative economic strategies are no more than paper exercises unless they generate the political will for radical change; and this means that they must be seen to build upon the economic power of workers through their Combine committees and the political power of local communities through their elected councils.

What all this means is that the various elements in an alternative economic strategy — National Enterprise Board, Planning Agreements, Import Controls and Planned Trade, Wealth Tax, Prices and Incomes Policies, Expansion of public health, education and social services — cannot be seen only as a set of instruments, a package of legislative measures for managing the economy at a higher level of productive employment. They won't even do that, as the record of the last Labour Government shows, unless every element in the strategy is built upon the knowledge and commitment of working people organised in unions at their workplace and in community associations where they live. Building a strategy in this way is not just a matter of making the speeches that create the links — no one does this better than Tony Benn. We need actually to develop the model which will link the needs that people express for themselves and the productive capacities of workers in ways that neither the old market model nor the command economy model can ensure.

I am going to suggest that some of the employment initiatives of local authorities are providing us with a first insight into a crucial aspect of the new model. The chief aim of the Local Enterprise Boards that a number of authorities are establishing is not to take over bankrupt companies nor even profitable enterprises — that is not, in any case, within their powers. It is to provide a whole range of supporting facilities, including financial aid for local enterprise and particularly for co-operative enterprise, that not only creates or maintains employment, but also seeks to meet the expressed social needs of the community. It is concerned, therefore, to encourage and support actions that come up from the people themselves rather than imposing from above a certain pattern of development and seeking to control it thereafter.

Of course, the power and resources of local authorities are limited by statute and can be removed at a stroke by a Minister with the support of Parliament. It may seem to be a weakness of the British constitution in a period of transitional struggle that all power is concentrated at the centre, but this might make much easier a total social transformation if such a change were willed by the people. Once power is centralised it is hard to decentralise. There is a danger of appearing to be two-faced about this — welcoming the power of Labour local Councils to advance socialist measures and preventing the power of Tory local councils to resist them. The fact is that there can be no security for a socialist transformation of society in any nation where central state power is inadequate to prevent the separatist tendencies of self-governing regions or self-governing economic enterprises. Devolution of power in Yugoslavia to the separate states, and to self-managed enterprises, has rendered the market once more the main determinant of resource allocation and has encouraged increased inequalities between states and between enterprises. Yet totally centralised power must be avoided. The political and economic model that provides for local enterprise and self-management within a national and international framework of planning has still to be developed.

None of this should derogate from the very great value, in a period struggle for change, of the exploration by local authorities of economic strategies that will both support local initiatives and help in defining national policies. The main advantage for popular power of the information revolution that computers and microelectronic controls have brought about, is that the planning that had previously to be done by bureaucratic authority can now be replaced by the popular selection of different options that each give a realistic matching of production possibilities and expressed needs on a national and international scale. When there is not one, but several alternative mixes of a range of goods and services that people can choose from within the limits of available resources, the power of central bureaucratic authority is greatly reduced. Within specified resource constraints provided by taxation and other legislated transfers to the rest of the economy, local authorities could be encouraged even now to develop their own economic plans linking the productive capacity of workers and the expressed needs of communities in their area. Such planning would help to solve one of the most intractable problems in a period of transition to a socialist order. This is the unequal productivity of different enterprises, plants and companies, which leads, in conditions of private accumulation, to natural trade union pressure for wage increases far beyond what can be met out of average levels of productivity throughout the whole country. If local authorities could derive funds not only from rates, but from the profits of high productivity enterprises in their area, subject to a system of equalisation between different areas, then the wage pressure in high productivity plants and industries could be eased.

Much of this discussion consists of speculation about the run-up to a radical transformation of the political economy of this country, and it may seem to some that this is a distant prospect. What it is designed to emphasise is that little progress will be made in the advance towards a radical change if this is not based on workers' plans for their own plants, companies and industries, and on local authorities' integration of these plans into their own range of social provision. To deepen the involvement of local people in the process of determination of needs it will be necessary to establish a more effective lower level of local government comprising roughly the numbers of people in a ward or housing estate, something of the order of 1000 families making forty to sixty wards in each authority.

In a book on *Resources and the Environment** I suggested some years ago that a first step towards decentralised decision making could be the establishment at national, regional, district and local level of Social Audit groups. Three related reasons were given for the concept of a Social Audit.

(a)   *educational* Until we begin to collect and to publicise information about the resources we have and their current use and abuse in waste and other anti-social developments, the understanding of the need for change will not exist. It is only necessary to cite the general ignorance that existed about the connection between H-bomb tests and radiation effects or between smoking and lung cancer to recognise the danger of current ignorance about the exhaustion rate of non-renewable fuels and minerals or the disturbance of ecological balance through the use of fertilisers, pesticides, etc.

---

*Spokesman, 1976, £5.50.

(b)   *agitation* Until groups of citizens seize upon particular examples of abuses and forms of waste, and demand their correction, the will for change will remain undeveloped. Conservation societies are proliferating, but what we know about social change in the past suggests that a massive concentration of human energy has to be generated to disturb the general acceptance of things as they are. The conditions for a revolutionary change are not only the break-down of old ways of doing things, but the crystallisation of groups of human beings around a new way of doing them.

(c)   *transformational* Unless such groups can grasp the actualities of the changes needed, the direction of change will be mistaken and the bridge-heads for the most crucial changes will not be seized. The trade unions are key groups in this respect today, because of the increased strength of their controls over their workplace conditions and their growing aspiration to extend such controls into full workers' self-management.

The success of the idea of such a Social Audit I concluded would probably depend on four considerations:

1.   the involvement of trade unions at plant level in the obtaining and analysing of information about their company's plans and resources;

2.   The widespread awareness that can be developed of the overall idea of the Social Audit as an instrument for exercising real control over our environment, through successfully adapting ourselves to its laws and necessities;

3.   the organisation at every level of Social Audit Groups, with some support from public funds but mainly depending upon people themselves at their place of work and residence, i.e. at the lowest level of all where the interest of the individual household and the local community find their essential interaction.

4.   the expansion of education opportunities to study how facts are collected and analysed and related to different conceptual frameworks, so that more and more people can form their own Social Audit groups, and "the educators" among the ordinary people can, as Marx put it, "become themselves educated".

Support for such groups could be a first claim on University and Polytechnic staffs. This could involve research work using unemployed Social Science graduates on STEP schemes for the first stages of investigation and surveying.

To illustrate this theme I give below two examples of approaches by Labour Councils to the creation of Local Enterprise Boards.

A Sheffield or South Yorkshire Enterprise Board

1. *Aims and functions*

    Authorities which have established or are in process of establishing boards of this nature, e.g. Manchester, Wigan, Southwark, Greenwich and the GLC, have done so by setting up companies with three general aims:

    (1)   to act as an executive arm for their employment and economic regeneration policies;

    (2)   to enable a wider range of functions to be performed beyond those conferred by statute on the authorities themselves;

    (3)   to decentralise responsibility "at arm's length" from the Council (as opposed to delegation of powers).

    The functions are in the main:

    to hold land, and construct (or convert) factories, own and lease plant and buildings, raise finance, make loans and grants, provide guarantees, employ staff, including expert advisers, planners and co-ordinators of local authority facilities.

2. *Legal Status and Vires*

    It appears from counsel opinion elsewhere that there are no legal objections to the following acts with the provisos indicated:

    (a)   setting up a company and paying costs of establishment, provided that land, goods and services would have to be sold to the company;

    (b)   widening the range of its functions beyond those open to a local authority, provided that the funds of the local authority are used only for those purposes covered by the source of the funds, e.g. Section 137 and Inner City Funds;

    (c)   placing councillors on the Board provided they are not paid a fee or have personal shares or a contract of employment (they could receive expenses as an "approved duty") and holding in the Council's hands a voting majority of shares;

    (d)   making grants of monies or loans at interest to the Company within the limits of Section 137 and of Inner City funds and of other funds, e.g. Manpower Services Commission funds and possibly EEC Social funds and Pension funds, subject to Pension Fund legislation.

3. *Geographical area of operation*

    The same arguments that led to the establishment of a

metropolitan county of South Yorkshire with four metropolitan districts might apply to the establishment of a Local Enterprise Board for the whole County. If agreement could be reached there would be evident advantages, in what is a single employment area, in establishing a Board for South Yorkshire by a consortium of the four district authorities and the County. But this is a political decision which can only be determined by discussion amongst the authorities themselves.

4.   *Manner of operation of the Board*

(a)   There is a very wide range of services and facilities which Local authorities provide to industrial and commercial enterprises and for which rates are paid. The Board would have power to influence investment and employment decisions of private companies through a whole range of local authority powers, as well as through providing or withholding finance. These powers include planning permission, rate rebates, industrial estate accommodation, housing, roads, sewerage, water supply, etc., education and training.

(b)   Provision of such local authority services and of finance by the authority(ies) can be made conditional upon a set of provisos concerned with employment and environmental policies — wages and conditions, equal opportunity against racial or sex discrimination, créche provision, number of new workers employed, product quality, respect for health and safety and environmental factors, information disclosure, import substitution etc.

(c)   Planning agreements could be drawn up between the Board, enterprises and the trade union representatives involved at different levels, such as were designed to ensure best employment practices, opening the books and favour investment planning in consultation with union representatives.

(d)   The Board would need to work closely with existing Local Authority agencies — Direct Works Departments, Purchasing organisations, Pension Funds, Industrial Estates, Employment Departments and Central government agencies — MSC — and local employers' organisations.

(e)   The Board could well concern itself with identifying social needs in the community and matching these with appropriate productive capacities and unemployed resources in the area.

5.   *Stimulation of Economic Development*
     Given all that has been said above, the main tasks of the
     Board would be to encourage and develop local initiatives
     from Trade Unions, Tenants' associations, CVS, Sports
     Clubs, Unemployed organisations, etc., pressure groups of all
     sorts, and above all, from potential and actual co-operative
     enterprises.
         This implies at least the following services being made
     available from the Board for co-operatives, municipal and
     private enterprise, such as are available to any plant in a large
     company.
     1.   Finance and banking.
     2.   Accountancy.
     3.   Sales, marketing and advertising.
     4.   Export agency.
     4.   Legal services.
     6.   Surveying and valuation.
     7.   Organisation and management.
     8.   Training and education.
     9.   Research and Development.
     10. Product design.
     11. Viability studies.
     12. Health and safety advice.

The Board would need to build up its own staff in all these areas
except in training and education where existing resources of Adult
Education Centres, FE Colleges, Polytechnics, Universities, Nor-
thern College, etc., could be called upon. In Research and Development also some assistance could be assumed to be available from
Universities and Polytechnics in forming a Science Park and in-
novatory centres.

6.   *Economic and Social Policy and the Enterprise Board*
     In order to co-ordinate the work of the Board and of the ex-
     isting initiating committees of the Council(s), it would seem
     to be essential to set up a small Economic Policy Group of
     councillors and their senior Economic Advisers and the chief
     officers of the Enterprise Board, with a professional staff to
     draw up plans and direct research.
         The location of the channels of communication between
     the Enterprise Board and Councillors' political decision mak-
     ing processes, would have to be most precisely determined;
     but this should not exclude maximum involvement in the con-

sultative process of the greatest possible range of voluntary organisations and special interest groups which might form the growth points for social action as well as of unions and employers.

Greater London Enterprise Board

1. *The Framework*

   The context for setting up a Greater London Enterprise Board (GLEB) framework is that it should be the main executive arm of the Council's industrial strategy for London. The strategy itself is intended to be researched and explored by a new Economic Planning Group and given consideration and authority through the Industry and Employment Committee. For this reason before outlining options for the framework of a GLEB this report sets out first the executive actions currently being persued by the Council and then the actions being taken by other agencies in the London area. The potential functions of a GLEB are then set against the legal, financial and organisational issues involved.

2. *Current GLC activities*

   Briefly, the Council has at present some 90 staff, mostly in the London Industrial Centre (50) undertaking industry and employment activities (other than research) with an overall budget in 1981/82 of £6m capital and loans and £5.8m (gross) revenue. Present activities in the field include:

   (i)   A practical client orientated advisory service, handling approximately 3,000 enquiries annually, of which about two-thirds (say 2,200) require detailed work and follow-up. The service is designed to assist in particular, with financial, statutory, industrial accommodation and staffing matters.

   (ii)   Marketing and promotion of London as a location for industry and commerce, both in the UK and overseas and in relation to (i) above, promotion of the services available from the London Industrial Centre.

   (iii) Provision of training courses for would-be and existing small businessmen and information and support activities directed especially to the expansion and development of market outlets.

   (iv)   Conversion and refurbishment of vacant or derelict properties for industrial use; 120 units should be completed in 1981/82.

(v)   Construction and promotion of the construction of small industrial units. Some 27 units (59,000 sq ft) are expected to be available in the current financial year and 32 units totalling 87,289 sq ft are planned for later years.

(vi) Identification of potential industrial sites with infrastructure or access problems and the development of solutions. Work is proceeding on Council-owned sites and investigations are in hand on three other sites.

(vii) Exploration of opportunities for growth related development in new and technology based sectors including the possibility of technology or science parks.

(viii) Activities under the Inner Urban Areas Act, including creation of industrial improvement areas in association with borough councils and loans and grants to businesses. Nine grants totalling £61,000 were approved in 1980/81.

(ix) Liaison with other groups in the field, including MSC, local employment groups, local business advice centres, partnership committees, and government departments.

3.   (i) *Local Boroughs*
Construction of industrial units; support for local business advice centres and direct provision of business assistance; local Trades Union unemployed workers' centres; local Trade Union resource centres; MSC schemes; development companies to provide financial help to industry; joint ventures; primary IUAA authorities; participation in training courses; limited marketing of Borough facilities.

(ii) *MSC*
The main roles are placing the unemployed; training and retraining; responsibility for YOP, CEP and WEEP; co-ordination of ITBs; provision of statistics and analyses of the labour market for government (and employers when requested); running the District Manpower consultative committees.

(iii) *Private Sector*
Local Chambers of Commerce and Industry, especially LCCI; Trades Councils; private sector involvement in business advice centres in association with the Boroughs; environment trusts on industrial estates (e.g. Park Royal).

4. *The Issues*

The issues raised by this brief survey of current activities in London by the Council and other agencies are, firstly, how far GLEB is to take over all the Council's present functions; second, to what degree GLEB will, having taken an initiative in a particular borough, hand over the project to the appropriate local agency if this is requested; third, how liaison is to be effective to avoid duplication; fourth, how far GLEB will need, wish and be able to take on some of the activities currently undertaken by other agencies, public or private.

5. *Additional Functions of GLEB‘*

There are three broad areas of new activities which are proposed for GLEB: the impetus for structural change in the economy by encouragement of co-operatives and municipal enterprise; the development of a much wider capital financing role, potentially involving public ownership, equity holding and risk taking on a considerable scale; a more far-reaching and intensive role of seeking out potential new investment and opportunities for expansion. In particular, it has been emphasised that a potential GLEB will seek to develop a 'balanced' portfolio of projects and investments, thus broadening the current principle of the Council being primarily a 'lender of last resort'. An enhanced level of property development is also proposed, including site acquisition, factory building or refurbishment and related activities.

6. For these additional functions the main issues are the resources to support them financially and the availability of suitably qualified personnel to execute them. On specific issues such as loan guarantees there are also questions as to the powers of the Council to act as may be required.

7. *Framework of a GLEB — Initial Position*

Organisation. From initial consultations it appears that if GLEB is to be an independent entity, then it would need to be a company. It has been suggested that a 'separate entity', separate, both physically and organisationally from the Council, could achieve a standing and broad effectiveness that could not be equalled by an 'in house' approach. From an initial consultation with Counsel it seems clear that a company could be set up to perform the functions currently undertaken by the Council and could be funded to some extent with Council finance, as are the present activities in this field. It seems probable that the administrative costs of a company could be covered by the Council making a contribution under Section 137(1) of the Local Government Act 1972. Counsel's opinion has been sought on a number of points which will be important in defining the organisation, control, finance and capabilities of a potential institution. The main issues are:

(a)   The extent to which the company's powers would need to be limited to GLC powers if GLC is a shareholder;

(b)   Whether GLC financial contributions would have to be limited for purposes within its powers;

(c)   How far grants of a capital nature and loans to the company would require Money Act provision;

(d)   Issues raised by the proposal to use a proportion of the Council's Superannuation Fund cash flow for investment in projects supported by GLEB;

(e)   The potential for the GLC to guarantee loans to GLEB or investments in projects supported by GLEB and to enter into deficit funding agreements which are, in effect, guarantees.

Counsel's opinion has just been received and the further detailed reports recommended below will be prepared in the light of that opinion (and any others which may prove to be necessary in specialist fields, e.g. company law).

The company would be subject to Corporation Tax, VAT and, on any property deals, DLT, and in any proposals these aspects would need to be covered in depth.

8.   *Organisation and Control*

(a)   If powers for the Council to give directions to the company were required, this could be achieved by including the proposal in the Memorandum and Articles of Association. The question of dealing with a contravention is being considered.

(b)   Elected members could act as directors of a GLEB company. This raises a number of issues, such as potential conflict of interest; the need for member/directors to be unpaid to avoid disqualification under LGA 1972; the

ability to claim expenses; the need for a member/direc-
tor not to vote on company matters considered by a
GLC committee or Council, all of which is being pursued. It is understood that if a company is set up, it is
envisaged that members would take up only one or two
places on the Board, the remainder being appointed
from representatives of the various sectors of the
economy.

(c)   There would need to be formal agreement on the
method of authorisation and monitoring of any GLC
financial contribution. There are precedents for this, for
instance, the agreement between Greater Manchester
Council and their development company.

9. If a company organisation were to be pursued then a structure
for executive action might be considered as three teams,
reflecting the three main investment functions, i.e.:

Business Development — co-operatives development;
municipal enterprise; advice to existing firms; small firms section; inward investment projects; specialist advice (e.g.
marketing, exporting, product development). (Investment to
promote strategic or structural change).

Finance — new ventures; IUAA activities. (General investment).

Project Development — Sites development requiring servicing from valuers, planners, road engineers etc., refurbishment of existing structures, development of nursery units.
(Investment to promote development).

Many of these activities are already undertaken within the
Council's departments as shown in paragraph 2.

10. *Other companies*

The Committee will, no doubt, be aware that other local
authorities in the country, including two London Boroughs
(Greenwich and Southwark) have already set up companies to
achieve a variety of objectives ranging from the very specific,
such as maximising use of MSC, CEP or YOP schemes
(Merseyside) to the very general such as furthering the
authority's objectives for economic development (Wigan).
The effectiveness of these companies has varied, and the
potential for avoiding government financial controls has, of
course, been affected since 31 March 1981.

11. If the Committee decides to agree in principle the establishment of a company to form the GLEB then three main stages of detailed work will be necessary. First, to establish the main approaches to the extent of powers, finance and functions and make proposals following staff consultation; second, following guidelines from the Committee on the approaches to be adopted, preparation of appropriate Memorandum and Articles of Association and detailed procedural proposals; third, final proposals for staffing and implementation.

12. As a first step *the Committee is asked to decide in principle* whether the proposal to set up a GLEB as a company, to perform the executive functions of the Council in economic development should be pursued. If so then:

   It is recommended that, following staff consultation detailed reports should be submitted covering:
   (i) the outcome of consultations on the issues raised in paragraph 7;
   (ii) methods for control of the activities and finance of the company, including composition of the board and the extent of authorisation for expenditure of Council money;
   (iii) the likely level of available finance from present resources;
   (iv) effects of proposals on the present staffing organisation and budgeting of economic development executive functions;
   (v) proposals for resolving the issues raised in paragraph 4 related to other organisations.

CHAPTER EIGHT

New Public Enterprise and Economic Planning

Stuart Holland

In the early 1970s many of us warned that a decade of de-industrialisation would occur unless we pursued radical policies for new public enterprise and planning. We were told such policies were unnecessary and damaging to our electoral chances. In 1973, the then leader of the parliamentary Labour Party sought to veto the proposals of Labour's National Executive Committee (NEC) for a wide ranging National Enterprise Board (NEB), taking on both Clause IV and Clause V of the Party's constitution since he had no power to veto a proposal from the NEC to Conference. In government, however, by 1975, both the NEB and Planning Agreements were gelded in cabinet, reducing means for new planning, public enterprise and industrial democracy to 'voluntary' status.

Meanwhile, a degree of disillusion with both the NEB and Planning Agreements emerged in some sections of the Labour Movement. Such disillusion was not universal. Some combine committees of shop stewards demanded the right to information and bargaining for changed forward planning of the kind which they should have had by right and by law if Planning Agreement powers had been introduced in legislation. Some saw that the so-called Planning Agreement with Chrysler was nothing of the kind, but rather a camouflage job on a management which had burned its profits in taking over Rootes and wanted to pull out of the enterprise. But the lack of powers for either new public enterprise or Planning Agreements, in legislation, defeated key efforts for mobilisation in combines such as those of Lucas Aerospace or Vickers.

So where do we stand now on Labour's policies for public enterprise and planning? Were they tried and failed, or did we fail to try them? How successful were the alternative policies of (SWP) Sector

Working Parties or the (NEDC) National Economic Development Committee 'talkshops' versus the 'workshops' of the NEB and Planning Agreements as shaped in opposition last time round? How successful also were the policies of industrial regeneration based on private initiative and public subsidy of private enterprise as pursued by the Labour Government from 1975 to 1979? Not least, what were the real aims for public enterprise and planning as shaped by Labour in the early 1970's and how do we adapt them to new dimensions of crisis in the British economy?

1. ECONOMIC POLICY AND PUBLIC ENTERPRISE

The 1974 manifesto stated the aims of new public enterprise to be: (1) investment stimulation; (2) employment creation; (3) export promotion and import substitution; (4) promotion of industrial efficiency; (5) the countering of monopoly power and (6) prevention of unacceptable foreign control of British industries.

In so doing the manifesto reflected the case for new public enterprise as argued in NEC committees and endorsed by the 1972 and 1973 Conferences. This paralleled some aspects of the arguments for 'first generation' public ownership, but added the new 'second generation' case for harnessing and transforming the role of multinational big business in the British economy (also reflected later in the NEC's Discussion Document 'International Big Business').

The six main 'new public enterprise' aims also were backed by other keys aims of re-mixing an unequally mixed economy, and planning the role of big business in both the private and public sectors through Planning Agreements. Attention was drawn to the fact that public enterprise was concentrated either in basic industries and services with high capital intensity and/or low export potential, or otherwise advanced high technology sectors (nuclear power, energy, aerospace) where private enterprise frequently would not venture the risk capital or would do so only on subsidised terms.

Overall, public enterprise, then as now, represented only just over a tenth of UK GDP.

Today we hear from the sirens of the SDP that the present mix in the economy is sacrosanct and crucial to our freedoms. But what in practice has that mixed economy delivered under private enterprise domination? The 1970s saw an unparalleled degeneration of industry in Britain. Private enterprise failed to achieve any of the six main aims scheduled for new public enterprise in Labour's 1974 manifesto:

(1) manufacturing investment in Britain has fallen persistently and is now ingloriously around its 1968 level;

(2) unemployment now is over 2.5 million, having hit 1.5 under a Labour government, with the main unemployment occurring in industry;

(3) export trade in manufacturing failed to respond to the massive devaluations of the mid-1970s (when sterling at one point was two thirds down on the 1971 value of the Deutsche Mark), while import penetration, especially from Japan and Europe has decimated whole sectors of industry;

(4) industrial efficiency is low through failure to reverse the 'defensive' investment posture of business in Britain and through an outwards investment 'offensive' by British based multinationals;

(5) little was done to counter monopoly power (through limits to the powers of the Price Commission) with big business mainly able to compensate itself for fallen sales by raised prices. The real profits of the top 25 firms increased by seventy per cent from 1969 to 1977 against an increase of only seven per cent for all industrial and commercial companies *(Economic Trends,* 1977, 1978);

(6) as against the aim of preventing foreign control of British industry the Labour government refused the offer of Chrysler's UK operations (with repayment of grants) and ended up bidding for engine plants from Ford, joint ventures with Honda etc.

Retrospect on the NEB

SDP spokesmen apparently see the NEB (now due for demise into a research and development organisation) as a part of the acceptable public sector. Many Labour spokesmen rightly demanded a different and more powerful NEB as a key part of Labour policy in the 1970s. For in reality, the NEB we got was not the NEB we drafted as a power house for the regeneration of British industry. In re-evaluating the role of public enterprise in the economy, it is crucial that we also frankly judge the limits of the NEB in practice.

Much of the force in the NEB proposals lay in claiming that indirect Keynesian instruments of intervention to achieve such aims (through tax, interest rate and fiscal policies) had been undermined by the trend to monopoly and the multinational spread of capital. The time period of investment and product planning in big business now ranges longer than the lifetime of most governments, and than budgets and tax and interest rate changes. The trade pattern of British companies based at home and exporting abroad also has given way to major foreign investment and the substitution of foreign production, in key markets, for export trade.

The basic data on the change in the economy since Keynes formulated macro-economic policies of demand management were stressed in the original case for the NEB. They included the increase in the share of the top 100 manufacturing companies from around a fifth to nearly half of net output between 1950 and 1970, with similar shares in their increase in employment; the command of half of visible export trade by only 75 firms, and a foreign production relative to visible export trade of 2:1 — some five times the ratio for countries such as Germany and Japan, who remained predominantly exporters of goods rather than enterprise.

It also is important to stress that the NEB was not conceived in isolation from other policies, and in particular Planning Agreements with 'certainly the top 100 manufacturing companies' (Labour's Programme 1973). If the NEB was intended to be the 'left hand' of Labour's industrial strategy, with more than an echo of Clause IV commitments on public ownership, Planning Agreements were intended as their 'right arm'. They were supposed to cover existing nationalised enterprise, new public ownership through the NEB and the remaining big league private enterprise (in the jargon of the time the Category 1 firms with £50 millions turnover or more at 1972 prices).

The NEB was intended to take a controlling public holding, depending on the size of the company, in from 20 to 25 of the top hundred manufacturing companies over a period of a full parliamentary term (Opposition Green Paper, The National Enterprise Board 1973). Later this was extended into a public stake in a major company in each of the 32 main industrial sectors covered by the Sector Working Parties (Labour's Programme 1976). The NEB 'push' was supposed to complement the Planning Agreements 'pull' on the remaining big league private companies, and to give an 'imperative' element to planning, while Planning Agreements — compulsory in principle — would or could remain both less than wholly imperative and more than merely indicative.

Workshops versus Talkshops

In this sense the NEB was supposed to play a key policy role. It was to go beyond the 'talk shops' of the NEDCs or SWPs into the 'workshops' of companies themselves. It was not conceived as simply a micro-economic instrument, but as a powerhouse in the major new economic structure of big business between the macro-economic level of government policy and aggregates and the microeconomic level of the remaining small scale, mainly national, price-taking rather than price-making companies which were being shrunk into the lower half or third of British industry. It was to bridge the macro-micro gap by what some of us identified as the new meso-economic sector between macro and micro-economics. (Greek: mesos — intermediate).

By such standards the NEB which transpired in reality was a different instrument. It fulfilled a role in British industrial policy, and especially in the first three of the eight main areas identified in Labour's Programme 1973, but not the key roles assigned to it by the Party or by the manifestoes in 1974. In practice, its role was the defence of jobs and markets rather than the offensive go-getting strategy assigned to it by Party policy. In crucial cases it underwrote failure rather than reinforced and promoted success. It has little net impact on trade; none on prices policy, virtually none on tackling multinational companies and next to none in promotion of industrial democracy.

One reason was the gelding of the powers of the NEB to take controlling holdings in major companies, with power of share acquisition. In practice, legislation denied the NEB even those powers allowed to a private company through a takeover bid, irrespective of the wishes of management of the company for which the bid was made. Takeovers, like Planning Agreements, had to be mutually agreed. By this one provision, embodied in the 1975 Industry Act, the NEB was transformed from a potential agent of real change in the economy to an assistance and salvage operation for problem companies. The change meant the difference between a socialist instrument for transforming economic power to a State capitalist instrument for reinforcing it.

Such a judgement remains valid even for that area of the market where the NEB took initiatives which created new enterprises. INMOS, NEXOS and the other 'Greek' ventures of the NEB into the production of micro-technology were worthwhile in themselves. But the conditions on which they were made were both small scale and reactive, if not reactionary. Britain needs a strong representation in the production of 'chip' technology, rather than simply in software. But we bought the technology by committing only £50 millions (as against £500 millions spent by the Japanese), while allowing terms which would literally create millionaires from the entrepreneurs concerned. We also managed the remarkable feat of ensuring that the first half of the NEBs investment in this area would be in California, an area not widely known as a UK problem region.

Degeneration and Salvage

Without doubt the inclusion of British Leyland in the category of NEB companies swamped it from the start, representing two thirds of its total employment and 85 per cent of its use of funds. Altogether, the NEB by the end of 1978 has some stake in 52 companies, but:

● Rolls Royce and ICL had already been nationalised or brought into the public sector through controlling holdings;
● Rolls Royce and British Leyland dominated the financial requirements of the NEB (around 90 per cent of committed funds);
● Alfred Herbert was never seriously 'turned round' nor launched on a major modernisation programme as a pacemaker in machine tools.

Thus the NEB never was in a position to play the major role envisaged for it as a vehicle which could help bridge the gap between macro and micro economic policy:

● its interventions were mainly reactive and defensive rather than actively offensive in promoting a broad wave of investment — thus there was no wider planning role as originally envisaged;
● through lack of a complementary Planning Agreements framework, there was no significant push-pull effect on other firms;
● there was no clear focus on big business of the 'meso-economic' kind, rather than pre-occupation with several, small micro-economic enterprises and dominance by three or four very large firms;
● there was virtually no conscious contribution to regional development policy, so that by 1977 the main regional offices established by the NEB were mainly turning down projects in the regions on a merchant bank type basis.

Besides this, the NEB played not only a reactive role in relation to the trades unions in its companies, but an increasingly reactionary role. The original Ryder Plan for BL was ambitious, and did involve a degree of participation by trades unions in its formulation. But this participation did not work both from 'top down' and 'base up' on an on-going basis. It carried little credibility on the shop floor that a genuinely 'new deal' had been started in the company.

The Godfather Effect

The result, especially from the appointment of Michael Edwardes as head of the company, was a new State 'godfather' effect in industrial relations. Tranches of NEB funds were forthcoming only if the unions would accept terms and conditions which increasingly were determined by management from above. Offers which the unions sometimes felt they should refuse included one dose of unemployment now in the leg or two later in the head. As opposed to the principle of pioneering new forms of industrial democracy and co-operation with the shopfloor, BL became a symptom of confrontation with the unions, leading to the sacking of Derek Robinson (who in fact had been criticised by his own senior TU colleagues for too much co-operation with some aspects of the Ryder Plan).

Overall, the NEB could be said to have made some contribution to the first three of the main aims established for it in Party and manifesto policy: i.e. job creation — though in the main, job defence; technological development — through the promotion of micro-electronics and investment promotion. But, in general, this intervention was partial, unplanned and parsimonious. The overall budget of only £1 billion for the first four years contrasted dramatically both with the sum of £1 billion a year demanded by the TUC through the 70's, and with the public subsidy of private capital undertaken by the last Labour government.

To put the NEB's funding in perspective, in addition to the fact of its 85 per cent allocation to BL, its £1 billion over *four* years contrasted with:

- £1 billion a year — rising to near £2 billions in 1979 — granted to the private corporate sector through tax relief on stock appreciation, introduced in the autumn of 1974;
- £1 billion scheduled for the competing FFI (Finance for Industry), which on the 'Lever Plan' was intended to make finance for industry available without the conditions of planning framework of the NEB;

In effect, the policies pursued with regard to the NEB were classic State capitalism, of the kind against which we warned in the original presentation of its proposals at the time of the 1973 Opposition Green Paper. It intervened to offset or underwrite failure in the private market on a partial, *ad hoc* basis, rather than to transform the working of the market through establishing a power house for new economic planning. It never seriously challenged the dominance of internal private criteria within its enterprise (with the partial exception of one overall estimate of the jobs indirectly dependent on BL which would be lost if BL itself were run down on a faster scale). It also failed to change the social relations of production at work, within enterprise, and give a major new role to labour and the trades union movement.

The issue of its personnel was symptomatic of these failures. No one associated with the formulation of the NEB proposals was directly associated with the NEB itself. 'Sound' businessmen dominate the management structure of the NEB, despite the representation of high level trades unionists in minority positions on its board. This was part and parcel of the exercise undertaken by the Labour government (despite notable opposition from some members) to ensure that the NEB personnel and their terms of reference would appease the City and the system, rather than dynamise and finance fundamental change in the performance of industry in Britain.

Overall Assessment

Political and economic judgements on the NEB saga are important for evaluating new forms of future public enterprise. In addition to those already made, we also should face the following:

1. that the time period between the publication of the original proposals and their endorsement in large part by Conference, followed by the February 1974 election was very short. Many activists in the movement had only an intuitive idea of what the proposals meant, and too few were aware of the key link between a powerful and wide-ranging NEB and the Planning Agreements system;

2. that some of the leadership of the Party saw the proposals either as unnecessary at the time, or too radical, or simply an indictment of their own policies in government in the 1960s, and thus not only did not support, but actively opposed them. On these grounds it could be said less that the NEB ideas was tried and failed, but that the government failed to try it on sufficient scale and with sufficient powers;

3. that while much of the NEB's activity was worthy enough in itself, it failed to stem the overall decline of industry in Britain through the decade. Of the 32 SWPs originally established, nearly all presided over a worsening of investment and import penetration by the time that they had identified what action should have been taken to stem or offset industrial decline in the seventies;

4. that the option considered originally by the Public Sector Working Group of the Party for more than one State holding company — focused in engineering, construction, banking and in-

surance respectively — might have proved more viable than a single holding company. Also, that the concept of re-introducing an institution called an Industrial Re-Organisation Corporation (IRC), to complement the NEB in industry, might have enabled a clearer distinction to be made between the NEB's envisaged role of promoting and reinforcing success and the IRC type role of reorganisation and re-structuring;

5. that the overall planning framework within which the NEB should operate and to which it should be accountable went by default between 1972 and 1974. Instead of either a transformed Treasury, which could have become Ministry of the Budget and Planning, or a Cabinet Committee for Economic Planning serviced by a Planning Commission, it was envisaged that the 'super Mintech' of the Department of Trade and Industry would play this role. But the DTI was broken up, with the result that the trade dimension was lost and the countervailance of the Treasury became more difficult.

Review and Preview

With hindsight, it is clear enough that the movement has taken on board several of these points already.

- the NEC now is committed to not only a rolling manifesto, but also to the publication of regular discussion documents behind Conference proposals which should be discussed by special policy conferences, as envisaged from later this year;
- the Party now is crucially concerned to evolve mechanisms which give greater accountability for what government does rather than what we say it will do, which can and should be complemented by more effective action for economic democracy and workers' control;
- it now is widely admitted that the compromise policies of voluntary extension of the public sector, and voluntary Planning Agreements have failed to stem Britain's industrial decline and import penetration;
- the Party now is committed to new public intervention in construction, banking and insurance, and health equipment and goods (through the National Health Corporation);
- the Party, from 1976, committed itself to a National Planning Commission and Cabinet Committee for Economic Planning, rather than a single ministry approach to industrial and other domestic economic policy.

Besides which, despite some bitter disappointments over

Labour's industrial policy from 1974 to 1979, the main issues put on the agenda in the early seventies, including the demand for a powerful NEB and obligatory Planning Agreements are still in the forefront of the formal demands for economic policy, as witnessed by the recent special conference of 1980.

Against this, however, it is a fact that many activists and many members of the public think that Labour's Alternative Economic Strategy is essentially a matter of import controls rather than a combination of new public enterprise, planning agreements and industrial democracy.

In effect, the imperatives for new economic policy in the later 1980s and 1990s will need to be more ambitious than import controls alone. We shall need controls over, not only import, but export trade (through direct intervention by public ownership and leverage on remaining big league private companies through Planning Agreements). This also needs to be related to the main aims of the Alternative Economic Strategy which include investment, jobs, prices and technology, as well as trade.

Current revaluation of our economic strategy also must take accounts of the 'third industrial revolution' in the form of minicomputers and processors, optics, photonics and the other new technologies assessed and in the Party's discussion document on Microelectronics. As stressed later in the argument on new dimensions to planning, and in contrast with the 1960s, investment today tends to displace rather than create jobs, and in both industry and services. We can no longer count on expanding private services to absorb jobs displaced in industry through new technologies.

Similarly, while import substitution is on the agenda through planned trade, the task of export promotion is more difficult than in 1973, before the OPEC price hikes and the over-reaction of governments who slammed on the brakes to make room for oil imports, pushing us with help from the IMF into 'beggar my neighbour' deflation. This is apart from the sometimes exaggerated, but nonetheless real, issue of retaliation in other markets against UK protection.

These new dimensions to already fundamental problems give more rather than less importance to the case for a major and wide-ranging new public sector in the British economy.

The essentials of the case for new public enterprise as argued in the Party have been simple and should remain so if that case is to gain new and wider support. They could be summarised as follows:

Private enterprise has failed the nation by showing itself unable to:

1. gain from the lowest real wages in Community Europe by investing in Britain on a major scale;
2. undertake a modernisation offensive rather than react to market change;
3. defend and transform traditional sectors in economic crisis rather than speculate in unproductive sectors such as property;
4. increase visible exports in key markets rather than export capital and jobs;
5. locate new employment in problem regions and areas (and especially now the inner city of metropolitan regions);
6. respond through new investment and enterprise to massive government rebates or handouts which have virtually abolished corporation tax.

New Public Enterprise

It might be argued in principle that such deficiencies of the private sector could be overcome through new planning mechanisms alone without the extension of the public sector.

However, new public enterprise will be crucial to the success of planning and demand management policies. Put simply, much of such planning and demand management is based on an assumed 'pull effect' on enterprise in the private sector. The failure of such a pull effect through Keynesian fiscal, monetary and exchange rate policies was one of the key reasons for decline of Keynesianism, even before Treasury mandarins got bitten by the monetarist virus. As simply, one of the key roles envisaged for new public enterprise since the early 1970s has been a 'push effect' on the supply side of the economy, capable of complementing macro demand management and planning mechanisms. Taken to extremes the push me-pull me syndrome goes full circle, since a broad wave of investment promoted by new public enterprise in individual sectors would generate demand effects through the economy. But reliance mainly, or exclusively, on 'pull' mechanism has been tried and has patently failed.

The case could be summarised as a 'broad wave' investment 'push' through the main industrial sectors of the economy based on public control through ownership of a leading firm or potential leader within individual sectors. In this sense the analysis is intersectoral, with emphasis on the external effects of changed behaviour by a range of enterprise on the economy, rather than simply a change in their internal management *per se*.

This case now is more important than ever, given the decade of de-industrialisation and investment decline which the British economy has suffered since it was first made.

Further, and still of relevance in the current context, the initial number of from twenty to twenty-five firms was derived from analysis of twenty-two main industrial sectors of activity in which public enterprise was under-represented or not represented, plus banking and insurance.

Not all of the enterprises concerned need have been actual leaders brought into public ownership. Some of today's swans are tomorrow's lame ducks, while cygnets at the lower end of the big league may need backing through public ownership to enable them to ride out takeover or 'no entry' tactics by established big business in the multinational sector. Ferranti was such a case in the NEB's portfolio.

Sometimes, as in the pharmaceutical industry, candidate firms select themselves for public ownership inasmuch as the market is dominated by foreign based multinational companies which could not easily be taken over (as opposed to some multinationals willing to have their British assets taken over, such as Chrysler in the mid-1970s).

A further case for public ownership is the scale of the dependence of an individual large firm on public spending for its revenue. This is especially the case in those enterprises highly dependent on provision of equipment on a large scale to the power generation and distribution sector, or in defence. The French Socialist Party has used and stressed precisely these arguments in its *Projet Socialiste*, which has been the policy background for the recent successful presidential election where candidate firms for public ownership were named (on the basis of the Common Programme list of 1972).

There is the further case of companies highly dependent for their success and private profit making on government purchasing such as computers, or public enterprise such as the remaining British owned motor vehicle industry.

This is in addition to the 'turnaround' from defensive to offensive corporate policy for individual large firms which are either are in difficulties because of inability to generate sufficient cash flow to modernise, or have been neglected by their multinational parent company which has focused resources on foreign investment.

But such specific factors, jointly with the case for import substitution and export promotion, should be considered in relation to overall planning for the promotion of a new wave of modernising investment in the UK economy, priorities for structural change and regional and urban re-distribution of jobs and income.

The criteria in this respect can be derived by working down from the needs of overall economic strategy to the level of the individual large firm and enterprise. The methodology of such a process has been elaborated in *The Socialist Challenge* as have the potential inter-sectoral linkage effects and 'positive multipliers' from a virtuous circle of investment expansion rather than the vicious circle of de-industrialisation and decline.

The Big Business Sector

A crucial factor is the focus of new public ownership on big rather than medium or small businesses or — at the borderline — medium firms with the potential for expansion. The distinction has been made elsewhere between the macro-economy (macros — large), the micro-economy (micros — small) and the new meso-economy of monopolistic and multi-national enterprise (mesos — intermediate).

It is in the new big business meso-economic sector that the thrust of new public enterrise should be focused, not simply because it is big in itself, but because it spans the gap between smaller micro enterprise and the macro aggregates of economic performance and policy. It is in this sector that leverage on the policies of individual firms can yield a new kind of 'mini-max' effect; i.e. when less than one per cent of enterprise in the system commands from a half to two thirds of activity, State intervention through public ownership can yield a maximal effect on macro economic performance with minimal direct involvement in terms of the overall number of firms in the economy.

Again, the French Socialist Party are clear, both on the need for a public enterprise base for their economic policies and the 'mini-max' role of the State. As they put it: "A public sector enlarged to the big business groups . . . will be the principal means of promoting and orientating industrial policy . . . The presence in strategic sectors of the economy of powerful and dynamic public enterprises in a planning framework will exert decisive growth promotion effects on the whole industrial fabric". *(Projet Socialiste,* p.194).

On the planning of public enterprise and its relation to the national planning framework, the French Socialists anticipate a Planning Agreement type policy of 'accords' focused on the arena of big business rather than small and medium and small firms. *(Projet Socialiste,* p.187).

The relation between new public enterprise and the planning process clearly would be crucial to the success of such enterprise in making a decisive contribution to resolving Britain's economic problem. The involvement of the trade unions in new public enterprise and the existing nationalised sector, and the role which both would play in a new planning process, would be of the first importance.

However, the role of individual public enterprises or public enterprise agencies also would be important. The Party is committed to various extensions of the public sector by successive Conference decisions, including (1) a major and enlarged role for an NEB and its regional agencies; (2) a National Health Corporation in medical supplies; (3) a National Construction Corporation based on one or more existing construction companies; (4) an enlarged National Oil Corporation plus restoration of the role of (5) British Aerospace, and (6) British Shipbuilders; as well as the defence and extension of the existing nationalised industries.

Several such public enterprises or public enterprise agencies would be very large if they met the needs for economic reconstruction with which Britain will be faced in the late 80s. Some will be preoccupied with what amount to salvage operations, including a sizeable part of the NEB and British Shipbuilders. Most of them should have an explicit regional structure for operational reasons and/or access other than exclusively 'through Whitehall'.

We should also consider whether there should not be some agencies primarily concerned with the salvage and rehabilitation. This was faced in the early 1970s when the case was argued that the NEB should be complemented by an agency with specific responsibilities for restructuring enterprise under public ownership over the medium term. At the time, partly out of awareness of the desire of the then Leader of the Party to re-introduce the Industrial Re-Organisation Corporation, it was considered that this might be a new IRC with a modified remit. But the proposal was ignored, and the NEB became *de facto* the nation's salvage agency.

Medium and Small Enterprises

This is not to say that new policies to socialise the small and medium firm sector are unimportant. They are more important than ever, granted the collapse of private entrepeneurship in small business and the implications of this for job loss in our inner city areas and problem regions.

Also we have to stress the extent to which Conservative mythology on 'the inheritance' principle in fact weakens small firms. When a first generation entrepreneur has stayed in the small league, the heir frequently is unwilling to take over the management of the company, or manages it with less drive and initiative than its founder. Diversification from owner-entrepreneurship to professional management poses classic problems in diversification and delegation for small firms. Typically, costs rise and profits fall in any attempt at transition, lining the firm up for either takeover or bankruptcy. Frequently, firms are too small to prove attractive to the big or medium league firms as takeover propositions. Therefore the best policy for a small entrepreneur often is 'disinvestment' for several years or not modernising plant and equipment while hanging on defensively to what markets are still available. This raises profit before the entrepreneur's retirement from the field and an asset stripping of the company.

Only new public and co-operative enterprise can respond effectively to this crisis for many small and medium firms. The 'enterprise zones' intended by the current Tory government, aiming to import the entrepreneurship of Singapore and South Korea to Liverpool and London are based on fantasy. South East Asian entrepreneurs benefit from wage levels a fifth or a tenth those in Britain, and labour relations ranging from refusal to recognise trade unions, through indirect repression to fascism.

The old style international division of labour of trade between different firms in different countries was supposed to ensure that we could compete against such low wages by higher efficiency or more technology. But the new multinational division of capital between the same companies in different countries has meant that multinational companies can combine the world's most modern technology with some of its cheapest labour in a manner giving them absolute advantage on world markets which enterprise zones in Britain will in no way effect.

Only new public and co-operative enterprise has the potential to offset these problems for small and medium enterprise in the economy. Such firms are mainly local and regional on their location. Workers' control can be more direct in small enterprise than in larger national and multinational companies.

But there is a false dichotomy being made by the Social Democrats and even some Labour supporters between new initiatives made only from 'the base up' versus old style initiatives from the 'top down'. Corporatism does not derive from bigness as such, but from the social and political relations of power with big business in the economy. Public enterprise, of itself, is no more socialist than planning, price controls or import controls. Socialism involves the socialisation of both ownership and control, allowing working people and their representatives in trade unions and politics to transform the use of resources in the economy.

A Plural Public Sector

If we are to transform the British economy and establish the dominance of public and social interests in the use of resources we therefore need to transform both ownership and control in both big and small business. We also will have to promote new planning mechanisms which make possible joint control by workers and government at both local and central government levels. When literally a few dozen companies dominate more than half our output, employment, pricing, investment and trade, we must ensure that central government is in a position to change the strategic command of the economy by such big business. When thousands of small firms are in crisis at the local level, we must place regional and local government bodies in a position to be able to modernise, diversify and adapt their role in the economy.

In itself, this represents the case for new public ownership and democratic planning at a variety of levels: national, regional and local. In essence this means demanding a new and more *plural* form of public enterprise intervention including:

1. outright ownership of some individual sectors of activity;
2. outright or controlling ownership in individual big business which itself in some cases means firms as big as some of the nationalised industries;
3. regional enterprise boards, rather than the salvage, reclamation and improvement agencies of the Scottish or Welsh Development Agency variety;
4. major municipal enterprise boards at the level of city regions, such as the Greater London Enterprise Board, now being pioneered by the incoming Labour GLC in London, and promoted elsewhere in cities such as Sheffield;
5. local enterprise agencies at the level of individual councils and boroughs.

Such new and more plural public enterprise at the national, regional and local level should be concerned with big, medium and smaller enterprise respectively. Clearly there should be inter-facing between these categories. If GEC or ICI were brought into public ownership, they would bring with them a range of individual companies and plant which are significant at the regional and local level.

But at the regional, metropolitan and borough level where Labour is already in control, we neither need nor should wait for the election of a Labour government to introduce new modes of public ownership and democratic control at the regional and local level. We may need to fight for the right to spend larger sums than anticipated under prevailing local authority legislation, or devise new ways of mobilising pension funds into directly productive activity, but in a range of areas we can begin and have begun the job already, without central government control.

Regional and Co-operative Enterprise

Further, just as the concept of a new public sector must be plural and wide ranging if it is to tackle the crisis in our cities and regions, so it should transcend conventional distinctions between public and co-operative enterprise, or central versus local control.

In *The Socialist Challenge* (Quartet Books, 1975) I pointed out that workers' control in big companies — some of which have as many subsidiaries as there are days in the year — could not be a matter of all workers all the time controlling all decisions affecting the enterprise. By definition, control worthy of the name rather than participation, must give workers control over the labour process and the workplace. But at the strategic level of the corporate plan of the enterprise, combine committees of shop stewards in different subsidiaries of the same company would need to bargain and share control mechanisms. Planning Agreements as a *process* of tripartite bargaining by unions with management and government were aimed to bridge the gap between tactical control at the level of the shop floor and the strategic control at the big company level. Thus outright control at individual plant level would necessarily mean shared or joint control at higher levels, i.e. control shared on labour's side between trade unionists in different subsidiaries and factories.

Similarly, there is no necessary conflict between outright control of a medium or small enterprise under co-operative ownership of its workers and joint venture arrangement with new regional, municipal or borough level public enterprise agencies. Just as Planning Agreements in the big business sector leave open the means of trade union representation to the workforce itself, so there are a variety of means by which workers' co-operatives can and should relate to agencies such as a new Scottish Enterprise Board, or metropolitan public enterprise agencies such as the Greater London Enterprise Board.

Thus an individual workers' co-operative at regional or local level may or may not decide to hold all of its share equity. It might choose to control 100 per cent but, on the other hand, it could decide to control only 51 per cent of the equity and invite a regional enterprise board to take up the remaining 49 per cent. This would have real advantages for a workers' co-operative which was facing the difficult transition period from traditional to modern markets since the principle of shareholding is that returns are only paid on equity when they are made, while the equity itself need not be repaid.

Alternatively, the co-operative might well decide that it should retain 100 per cent of the equity in the enterprise, and enter into a loan relationship with the regional enterprise board, judging that its economic potential was such that it would be able both to repay the loan and meet the interest on it. Clearly if the regional enterprise board were able to give grants to workers' co-operatives, or combine grants with loans, the workers would wish to opt for such an arrangement. Similarly, if the sums were very large — such as could well be the case if such new ventures were to make a major impact on local employment — the regional or local authority might well wish to re-cycle money from one firm to another and push for a loan relationship.

The individual options are less important than to recognise that there are options, with a wide range of alternatives crossing frontiers in conventional thinking on the public and co-operative sector. We need flexibility, and new modes of public intervention if we are serious about transforming job loss and unemployment in inner cities and problem regions. Perhaps especially in the co-operative sector, as recommended by the Party's discussion document on 'Workers' Co-operatives', we should be thinking of new dimensions to our overall strategy, rather than closing options onto single agencies such as the Co-operative Development Agency or NEB regional boards. For one of the strongest features of a plural approach is quite simply that if workers' initiatives meet no adequate response at one level (e.g. regional) they have others open to them elsewhere (e.g. national or local).

2. THE FINANCIAL INSTITUTIONS

In addition, there is the still critical issue of the scope and scale for public ownership of financial institutions in Britain.

Finance Capital

The basic scenario is clear enough. The Tories talk of competition while the monopoly trend proceeds apace. When Adam Smith wrote *The Wealth of Nations* in the 18th century, there were some 350 deposit banks in the United Kingdom. When David Ricardo wrote his *Principles of Economics* in the early 19th century, this had increased to some 450 independent banks. After successive banking crises in the intervening century, but especially since the end of the Second World War, this had been reduced to the concentration of 85 per cent of deposit banking in the hands of four banks. Competition comes in the colour of credit cards and who can collar the largest share of the rising professional class while they are still students, rather than in terms of credit or bank charges. Quit Lloyds for the Midland in your home town and you may gain a new overdraft from a new manager, but not new terms for your personal finance.

Meanwhile, a plethora of so-called 'merchant banks' — in practice investment and finance agencies — in the City of London, dominate the lending market to big business in Britain and abroad. Their role has become crucial to the finance capital sector because of the failure of the British stock market to meet the needs of British industry. For the last ten years the stock market in Britain has financed less than five per cent of the investment needs of industry in Britain. More than 85 per cent of the finance it raises is located in investment projects abroad. The main market for investment in British private business comes from the pension and insurance funds. By the mid-1970s concentration in insurance, had proceeded apace, with the top 10 companies accounting for 80 per cent of worldwide premium income. By the late 70s over half of the pension funds' assets were in the form of company securities. Lloyds alone accounted for some two thirds of the world's insurance and re-insurance market.

The financial institutions as a whole were estimated to have increased their share of UK ordinary shares from around a fifth in 1957 to 50 per cent by 1978. This paralleled the increase over the same period in the share of the top 100 companies in manufacturing output from around a fifth to nearly a half. By the end of 1978 the financial institutions also held just under half of listed UK company loan capital and three quarters of listed UK preference shares, as well as about two thirds of listed public sector securities. The pension funds and insurance companies between them controlled nearly two fifths of UK ordinary shares at the end of the 1970s. (Wilson Report on *The Functioning of the Financial Institutions,* 1980).

The rise of the pension funds has been dramatic. Membership of pension schemes has risen, increasing from 3 million employees in 1936 to 11½ million in 1975. Both pension funds and insurance companies between them account for a massive annual cash flow, around £8½ billion in 1978, all of which were seeking some kind of profitable outlet.

Harold Wilson was wholly wrong in claiming in the first parliamentary debate on his report that British industry already had been 'nationalised' by such an increase in the shareholdings of pension funds and insurance companies. He was also wrong in criticising Labour Party policy as having seen a lack of finance for industry in the early 1970s, when it recommended the major increase in public holdings in industry which his government refused to undertake. When public funds through pensions and insurance schemes remain under private control, they still are within the private finance capital system, subject to all its contradictions of failing to finance industry in Britain, and seeking profitable outlets in unproductive sectors of the economy such as property, or foreign investment.

But both the nature and structure of financial institutions in Britain today pose problems for the Labour movement. The call for public ownership of the financial institutions does not meet with a majority response from many unionists in the institutions themselves. Proposals to compensate owners on the basis of need have not yet been clearly matched by proposals for an alternative structure for financing pensions for those trade unionists who have invested in such funds.

Public Finance

Nationalisation of financial institutions is not a socialist measure *per se*. Where considered necessary, either in response to financial crisis or as a punitive measure for collaboration, right of centre or fascist governments have nationalised the main deposit banks in the system, as in post-war France or pre-war Italy.

In France today, under the new socialist government, there is a clear commitment to complete this process, both by extending public ownership and socialising control over financial institutions. But the structure of French finance is different from that in Britain. A much greater use has been made of personal savings for industrial and other investment through the post office savings system and the Caisse des Dêpots et Consignations. Also, the Ministry of Finance in France has been far more concerned to schedule finance into investment than has been the Treasury in Britain, which has fought to prevent specific use of particular funds in any kind of planning framework.

If we are to transform the role of finance capital in the British economy, and ensure the use of finance for public and social, rather than merely private ends, we need to recognise both the plurality of the various parts of the financial system, and the importance of ensuring transformed control of the use of resources. Otherwise, we could simply 'statise' ownership without socialising control.

A National Investment Board

A recent proposal from the TUC has been for the establishment of a National Investment Board to channel funds from the financial institutions into productive investment. This is an important proposal which not only has identified the failure of the private sector to finance investment in Britain, but also stresses the importance of productive investment as such.

The emphasis is crucial if we take account of the value-creating sectors of activity in the economy — in industry — and the comparative priority which an incoming Labour government will need to attach to the creation of wealth rather than the compensation of the already wealthy. It also has the advantage of simplicity, proposing a single agency for the channelling of funds from the financial to the productive sector.

Compensation of the wealthy could of course be avoided by a long overdue measure in Labour government policy — the introduction of a wealth tax. If similar to the tax which the rest of us pay, through PAYE, such a wealth tax could deduct at source — before fuller compensation — those sums which otherwise would disappear into the maw of tax avoidance schemes and tax havens. Such a wealth tax clearly would be critical to the success of any measures seeking to bring into public ownership a major share of the productive sectors of British industry.

However, any National Investment Board able to transform finance into investment in the later 1980s should fulfil the following requirements:

● command of sufficient funds to ensure finance for both economic and social investment programmes (in contrast with the present TUC proposal which is concerned only with industrial finance);

● a wide ranging remit, backed by legislative sanction, sufficient to bring within its scope private financial institutions, including not only the pension and insurance funds — as already proposed by the TUC — but also the major deposit banks and the merchant banks and finance houses;

● a direct relationship with economic planning, and the scheduling of finance to specific areas of the economy in accordance with clearly established policy priorities;

- specific directives from government instructing it to undertake the direction of funds to individual projects or sectors of activity and to make real its planning function;

- accountability both to the government itself (preferably through a Cabinet Committee for Economic Planning, even if an individual minister is responsible for its management), in contrast with the apparently quango-type arrangement considered at present by the TUC.

- the power to extend the scope of such an agency to take account of changing needs and circumstances.

Ironically, similar powers are available already to any government willing to use the terms of the Bank of England Nationalisation Act 1946, which in effect, gives the Chancellor of the Exchequer the power to instruct the Governor of the Bank to oblige the private banks to do whatever he thinks fit. A bill reinforcing and extending the 1946 Act would be sufficient to transform the role of the private finance sector in the British economy.

Clearly, there would be opposition to such a proposal from the financial institutions themselves, from the press and some other political parties. But, in a real sense, such an extension of public power into the finance sector is the minimum which would be necessary for the kind of central change which we need to ensure in the scheduling of savings into investment in the British economy.

Such a measure does not rule out the extension of public ownership into the financial institutions. Nor does it exclude Planning Agreement type arrangements with the financial sector over that part of its activities not covered by a National Investment Board. But it would give us the means — jointly with scheduling of oil revenues into investment — to overcome the divorce between finance and industrial capital in the system, and to make a radical shift in the use of funds in the economy.

This still leaves open the issue of ownership of the top four clearing banks, insurance companies and merchant banks and investment houses. When the 1976 Conference resolution on public ownership of the main financial institutions was passed, this was with the abstention of many unions and with a commitment from the National Executive that the issue would be discussed with them, in particular the unions in the financial sector.

The 1979 Report of the National Executive made four main recommendations:

1. An Investment Reserve Fund by which companies would deposit a percentage of their pre-tax profits with the Bank of England;
2. A rationalisation and merger of the existing public savings institutions — essentially the Giro and National Savings — into one new institution;
3. Public ownership of the four main clearing banks, plus the top seven insurance companies and one merchant bank;
4. A reform of the powers and terms of reference of the Bank of England.

The Investment Fund Scheme

The Investment Reserve Fund is different from the National Investment Board proposed by the TUC in that it would involve companies in the non-financial sector depositing funds with the Bank of England, rather than a mechanism such as the NIB which anticipates channelling financial sector funds into other activities. It is complementary to the National Investment Board proposal and offers considerable potential for gaining leverage over the use of funds by big business in the system. Put simply, such funds could be re-allocated to the companies in the big business sector as and when they undertook Planning Agreement commitments.

The effectiveness of the Investment Reserve Fund scheme would, in part, depend on the fourth recommendation from the 1979 Report: i.e. reform of the Bank of England. Certainly there is a strong case for claiming that the Bank of England so far has served the City and the financial institutions rather than served the people and the nation. Anecdote after anecdote on visits from the Governor of the Bank to Prime Ministers, telling them with regret that Labour could not have its public spending programmes without a collapse of sterling, illustrate the extent to which the Bank of England took over Labour governments rather than Labour from 1946 taking over the Bank. If the Investment Reserve Fund is in practice to work effectively, like the proposed National Investment Board, its main funding operations should be subject to the control of the Cabinet Committee for Economic Planning.

The Banks and Insurance Companies

Rationalisation of the Giro and the National Savings scheme is not notably contentious. The ownership of the four main clearing banks and the main insurance companies has caused more controversy. Unlike the other proposals they could involve very sizeable sums if their value was compensated at full rate, estimated at some £5 billions at 1979 prices. As already stressed, the combination of compensation with a wealth tax levied at source — i.e. deducted from compensation before it is paid — could have a considerable effect in reducing compensation payments. Also, it should be borne in mind that the 1945-51 Labour Government undertook compensation programmes for nationalisation at that time which, in 1979 prices, would have amounted to nearly £20 billions. Further, the figure of £5 billions compensation also has to be put against the £8½ billions annual income flowing to the pension funds and insurance companies at the end of the 1970s.

Besides, there is a clear net gain from bringing into public ownership those financial institutions which have major shareholdings in the industrial and commercial sector. The main seven or ten insurance companies in public ownership would bring with them a range of shares in key industrial and commercial companies by virtue of the fact that these institutions have tended to play safe in their investment portfolios, and favoured large rather than small enterprise.

It is evident that the Labour movement needs to decide clearly and soon on the scale of the ownership which it intends to make in the financial sector if we are to avoid the situation of the early seventies where we proposed a major stake in the industrial sector of the economy in what proved to be less than twelve months before a general election. But in both terms of cash value, and the leverage which this would permit over the economy as a whole, it is clear that there is a very strong case for endorsing the proposals of the 1979 Conference statement.

For those who claim that such proposals would divide the movement or deter electors, we should bear in mind that this government, with its liaison with finance capital, is allowing more than £1 billions gross to leave this country every three months of the year, as a consequence in part of its abolition of exchange controls. We also can point with reason to what has recently happened in France, where a government of the Left with a major commitment to public ownership of all financial institutions has gained a sweeping majority in the country. If some argue that this is irrelevant to what happens here, we should take account of registered unemployment, now approaching 3 millions, a higher youth unemployment than at any time, including the 1930s, and take our case for a new deal on finance and the economy to working people themselves.

3. NEW PLANNING PERSPECTIVES

'Plan' is a four-letter word. Like any word, its meaning also depends on its use. Some countries, like the Netherlands, have long-term plans which amount simply to forecasts; others, like France, have medium-term plans which now mask liberalisation and a return to market forces; others, like West Germany, claim not to plan, yet co-ordinate finance, investment and production to a high degree behind closed doors.

'Planning' by whatever name, nonetheless enjoyed considerable vogue in the 1960s, both in Britain and elsewhere. The French model of 'indicative planning' was exported to other countries without either the institutional or policy environment which had made it an effective vehicle of national reconstruction in the previous decade. In the 1970s, by contrast, the flight from planning and planned commitments was dramatic.

This flight from planning followed the OPEC price rises from 1973, which themselves followed a period of marked inflation in commodity and other prices, which in turn followed a period of declining capital accumulation and profit in countries with so-called indicative plans. The collapse of planning was closely linked to the breakdown of the international trade and payments system, and to the demise of Keynesian economics in national chancelleries and treasuries.

Part of the problem lay in the undermining of the Keynesian demand framework for planning policies by changes in the structure of supply. Predominantly small scale national enterprise in the immediate postwar period had by the 1970s given way to the dominance of multinational big business in production, distribution and trade.

Planners in France, Belgium and Italy had sought to counter this by evolving new planning instruments focused on big business in the intermediate or 'mesoeconomic' sector between macro aggregates and the small scale microeconomic firm of conventional model.

New planning methods in France and Belgium played a role in the formulation of counterpart Planning Agreements as a new dimension to planning in Labour Party policy perspectives.

However, as stressed by the heads of the Belgian and Italian planning offices at the time, and by the then director of the planning division — and later Finance Minister — in France (Fourcade), effective harnessing of the big business sector in economic planning depended on real powers of strategic control which were lacking in all three countries. French planners had been notorious, in Andrew Shonfield's words, as "part industrial consultants, part bankers and part plain bullies". But their sanctions through selective credit and public regulation were diminished by EEC entry and trade liberalisation.

One response in all three countries was to build up complementary public enterprise agencies in all three countries: the SNI (National Investment Corporation) in Belgium; IDI (the Industrial Development Institute) in France, and IRI and ENI (the Industrial Reconstruction Institute and National Hydrocarbons Corporation) in Italy.

Considerable success on a pre-existing public enterprise base was achieved in Italy in both investment promotion, job location in problem regions, and countervailing foreign multinationals, although Italian public enterprise neither was sufficiently wide ranging nor planned to counter the economic crisis of the 1970's. In Belgium and France the public enterprise response was both too little and too late to gain an effective lever in investment or trade. In Italy itself, public enterprise was still too limited, and too concentrated in basic industry and services, to yield a decisive macroeconomic influence.

Planning as both an issue and option for a future Labour government has been questioned by some people in view of its relative failure between 1964-70 and 1974-79 at, home, and the dominance of monetarism today.

But monetarism in the domestic arena, through de-planning, decontrol and dis-engagement of the State is in a crisis more patent and more transparent than the passive, reactive 'planning' of either Centre-Right governments abroad or Labour governments at home.

Nationally, monetarism and *laissez-faire* are in contradiction, since public spending mainly sustains rather than drains the private sector. High interest rates strangle those firms who have not been liquidated by the collapse in demand.

Internationally, monetarism has resulted in beggar-my-neighbour deflation on a global scale. No one needs a Nobel prize to see that one country's imports are other countries' exports, nor that the philosophy of cut, cut and cut again in Europe, North America and elsewhere now is collapsing world trade.

Both macro and micro policy remain crucial in government economic policy. The future growth of demand and intervention is crucial to the fate of small and bit business alike. Similarly, exchange rate changes still influence the trade of the shrinking microeconomic sector of small, national firms now representing some third of our export trade. But both macro and micro policy now depends on what we do or do not do in the big business sector.

The institutional problems and prospects of planning cannot be avoided. Too much detailed intervention in too many areas pre-empts ministerial and administrative resources and results in partial, imbalanced or counter-productive action. Likewise, inter-relations between international, national, regional and local action need to be both co-ordinated and devolved in key respects if planning is not to over-reach itself and become discredited.

Planning Priorities

Non-planning, whether in the form of passive State reaction to problems as they emerge, or lunatic *laissez-faire* such as pursued by the current government, cannot forecast, far less change, the economic future.

Planning from above, through technocratic élites and a liaison mainly between big business and government, will serve the short term interests of large capital, but impose the long term burden of economic and social change on labour and working people.

If we are to cope with the current economic crisis and the impending crisis to come, we cannot do so by imagining a return to either the 1960s or 1970s. We shall need to shape and specify the aims and use of resources on an unprecedented scale. We shall need to 're-mix' both the spending and supply sides of the economy by major changes in the public sector able to give us leverage on remaining big league private enterprise, and planning gains for the small firm sector.

Structural Planning

Such *structural* planning will need to cope with:

- stemming *de*-industrialisation in given sectors, where the analysis, at least in part, has been made by the Neddies and Sector Working Parties, plus trade unions;
- promoting *re*-industrialisation in some sectors where the private sector either has failed or been run down by multinational capital, where less analysis has been done, but the essential target will be recovering former production and markets with new technologies;
- channelling savings into investment at home rather than abroad and in productive rather than unproductive sectors, with special regard to the resources of pension fund and bank finance;
- relating trade planning and import substitution/export promotion to industrial re-structuring and regeneration;
- relating reflation of demand through public spending to price controls adequate to broadly ensure that increased cash flow to

enterprise, and reduced unit costs, are matched by price reductions.

Social Planning

Also, *social* planning will need to include:

- targets for the defence and extension of public spending in housing, health, education, social services, covered by a combination of effective corporation tax and oil revenues (indirectly contributing to increased sales in the enterprise sector and reduced unit costs);
- on-going information, available to trades unions and the public, on the probable incidence of technical progress on employment;
- involvement of trades unions at company and sector level in the rate of introducing new technologies, including flexible negotiation of conditions appropriate to individual firms and sectors on the introduction of a 35-hour week, 35-week year, or whatever agreeable in terms of reduced working time;
- an enlargement of the concept of the social wage to a concept of social income, including both increased pay for less working time as productivity permits, and the right to social income in a wider sense of services not paid directly by users (including feasibly, certain public transport services, a proportion of gas, electricity etc.);
- social negotiation by trades unions of the use of resources at company level, and their involvement in planning as a process of social negotiation of changed options for the use of resources in the economy.

Spatial Planning

Spatial planning will need to include:

- the broad regional distribution of investment and employment to ensure a relative balance in the location of resources and jobs;
- a relative balance in the distribution of activity by main economic sectors of industry and services, including the public and private sectors;
- urban planning, including provision for employment opportunities at whatever reduced level of hours or weeks, in inner city areas;
- transport planning, including not only cost benefit criteria, but also a shift from the private to the public sectors;
- environmental planning, including both reduction of pollution from road transport and new planning criteria based on social

need in planning enquiries and procedures (homes versus offices
in some areas, more office employment in others etc.).

Planning Means

If the above aspects of structural, social and spatial planning seems
ambitious, the means for effective intervention are available and
feasible if we match new public enterprise and planning processes
to the changed structure of economic power on the supply side of
the economy.

A critical factor in the feasibility of planning lies in the strategy
tactics distinction.

Central government should in principle be concerned essentially
with *strategic* planning issues; individual enterprise and local
government can feasibly be concerned with the *tactical* planning of
implementation.

The frontier between strategic and tactical issues is not rigid. On
occasion central government could and should be concerned with
tactical planning which fundamentally affects overall strategy;
similarly trade unions should be involved both with broad planning
strategy (mainly through national representatives) as well as tactical
options at the level of local government or individual companies.

Nonetheless, the transformed structure in the economy can be
harnessed in favour of effective planning. For instance, the figures
previously given on the command of the economy by a few firms
mean that less than one per cent of the enterprises in Britain today
control more than half of the economy.

Central government intervention, jointly with trade union
bargaining, on this minimal number of firms in the private and new
public sector could yield 'mini-max' gains if effectively planned,
i.e. a maximal impact on the economy through a minimal —
though decisive — central intervention.

Such planning should broadly distinguish between the
macroeconomic, mesoeconomic and microeconomic differences in
the contemporary economy, on the following lines:

*Macro*economic planning must be concerned with the broad and
big aggregates of economic activity, including:

consistency between the targets for the main economic objectives, including saving and investment, production and consumption, imports and exports, prices, costs and productivity
etc.;
overall shifts in the use of broad resources, including taxation
and finance of new investment or public consumption;
interest rate and credit policy, which should be based on both

direct and indirect criteria (e.g. a low interest rate and credit policy in 'paid for' by increased tax from those employed, corporate profits and VAT in an expanding economy);

exchange rate policy, without over-estimating the export potential of devaluation (now substantially qualified by multinational companies), nor under-estimating the role of the exchange rate in import and domestic price levels.

*Meso*economic policy focused essentially on the big and multinational enterprise in the economy, including:

new procedures for accounting the activity of such big business in a forward planning framework, against standard national accounts criteria;

complementary powers obliging such big business to present its accounts to government in a manner making possible forward information, which then could be incorporated in input-output accounting;

introduction of the sectoral, social and spatial dimensions of the activities of such big business, which represent so large a share of the economy (in the above senses of structural, social and spatial distribution);

national public enterprise in this big business sector to contribute particularly to the push effect on the supply side of the economy;

Planning Agreements between government, unions and management in such big business in both the public and private sectors, industry, finance, construction etc.;

Conscious relation of the role of such mesoeconomic enterprise to macroeconomic planning and the microeconomic enterprises which supply them as sub-contractors.

*Micro*economic policy concerning essentially the smaller, national enterprises in the economy, including:

positive discrimination to offset the monopoly trend through provision that a given proportion of public spending should benefit smaller enterprise (as already practised in the United States);

a microeconomic dimension to Planning Agreements with big business, concerned to ensure where possible that smaller firms in less developed regions or inner city areas gain sub-contracting from such big business;

a re-mix of local economies, where — as already stressed — municipal enterprise such as that scheduled for the Greater London Enterprise Board can intervene to protect, promote and provide demand for smaller firms through local finance, public purchasing etc.;

provision for the translation of smaller private companies into local workers' co-operatives, on the lines scheduled in the relevant Party proposals for co-operatives.

Institutions

Such planning, involving both the demand and supply sides of the economy, rather than Keynesian demand or Friedmanite supply factors, would need to learn from available negative and positive experience here an in other countries.

At one level we could well take a leaf from the Japanese, who responded to the specific crisis of the early 1970s by expanding, rather than contracting, their economy, and bringing forward to the late 1970s those technologies which otherwise would only have been employed in the 1980s.

Japanese planning already is based on the so-called mesoeconomic sector in its emphasis on big business or zaibatsus. But it also is integrated through a powerful trade and industry ministry (MITI) and a hitherto effective social consensus based on guaranteed lifetime employment for labour, rather than the threat of the dole.

Closer European models suggest that the concentration of planning responsibilities in one government department depends on cultural and élite factors which we neither could readily emulate, nor should necessarily endorse.

The relatively effective planning in the French Ministry of Finance and Economy up to 1963 depended essentially on a combination of élite cadres (from the École Nationale d'Administration and the Polytechniques) and weak governments during the period of the Fourth Republic, when officials were considerably more permanent than planning ministers.

Britain's 1960s experience of division of responsibility between the Treasury (allegedly responsible for short term policy) and the Department of Economic Affairs (for medium term planning) suggested two possibilities for planning institutions. Either the Treasury could be transformed into a Planning Ministry, or the institutional planning framework should be divided between the spending and sponsor ministries as a whole.

In practice the one path to avoid is division of short and medium term responsibilities between two ministries alone. In reality the medium term is reached through the short term, and the Treasury is responsible for short-term policy.

The institutional evidence from the British case strongly suggests that Party policy currently is on appropriate lines in recommending a ministerial Cabinet Committee for Economic Planning, where individual ministers and departments would be serviced by a National Planning Committtion.

The political case for a Cabinet Committee for Economic Planning, backed by a National Planning Commission relates to the scale of crisis which we shall inherit — considerably greater and more profound than that inherited in 1974.

Essentially, to countervail short term pressures and the *rigor mortis* of past othodoxies, funding ministers should be countervailed by spending ministers in an informed debate on new options for resource distribution. Moving beyond Keynesian planning (or monetarist de-planning) will need moves beyond classic spring or autumn budgets as the main instruments of resource allocation. Some monthly meetings of a Cabinet Committee for Economic Planning would be more important than others; bi-monthly meetings might suffice. But the main decisions should be bargained and shared at such a level, preferably chaired by the Prime Minister or a delegate minister and not by Treasury ministers.

Similarly, while a National Planning Commission should be responsible to the Prime Minister, individual cabinet ministers should have access to its forecasts, evaluations of options etc., and be able to request analysis from it relating to the overall planning strategy of the government. Individual ministers also should be able to employ planning staffs in their own departments, preferably combining 'insiders' and 'outsiders' on the French cabinet' system.

For similar reasons, Planning Agreements and responsibility for public enterprise should not be concentrated in one or two ministries only (as still considered by some in advocating a Ministry of Nationalised Industries).

If planning and new public enterprise are to play a strategic role in changing the future, rather than forecasting and underwriting failure, they will need to range through the broad spectrum of government decision making.

Thus, as the Coal Board and the BNOC are at present responsible to the Department of Energy, and the NEB to the Department of Industry, the new National Health Corporation scheduled in Party policy should be responsible to the DHSS, the new National Construction Corporation to the Department of Environment, a National Investment Board responsible for channelling finance from insurance and pension funds responsible to the Treasury etc.

Planning Agreements with big business should be co-ordinated

with macroeconomic objectives between individual mini-
sters/ministries, and the Cabinet Committee for Economic Planning. But the trade dimensions of such Agreements should be handled directly by the Department of Trade, employment by the
Department of Employment, investment and technology by the
Department of Industry, prices by Industry or Trade or a separate
department for Prices and Consumer Affairs if considered appropriate etc.

This makes practical sense inasmuch as not every Planning
Agreement with big business would be seeking change in every
aspect of the company's corporate plan. Export promotion and import substitution would be more important in some sectors and
companies than others; investment modernisation in some sectors
and companies would have more priority than others etc. Joint
negotiation of Agreements with key companies by ministers or officials from more than one department also would give more weight
to the policy.

The NEDC or SWP sector framework for information and
forecasting should continue to play a role in the planning process,
with the information co-ordinated through the National Planning
Commission. The Commission in turn should have a 'preferential'
relationship with the Central Statistical Office, and the latter
responsible for processing the sectoral information required from
big business through the Planning Agreements process.

Time Horizons

Granted the disbandment by the current Conservative government
of key planning staff, as well as the exchange control division in the
Bank of England, plus the new information and procedures anticipated for future planning, it is evident that the 'full' planning
process could not be started from the first day of an incoming
Labour government.

It also is clear that if Labour's future planning really is to change
the use of resources, stem de-industrialisation, re-industrialise,
reflate demand, reduce price inflation and redistribute jobs and income between sectors, regions and social classes, it will need to
work towards specific long term objectives on the shape of a changed economy and society.

It further is clear that planning procedure must be sufficiently
flexible to take account of changing circumstances in the overall
economic environment, and the needs of the key economic 'actors'
in the system. Accommodation to circumstances, modification and
change must be inbuilt into the process or it will fail.

But the short, medium and long term dimensions of the planning process should be conceived and institutionalised in a complementary framework. We cannot afford unrelated and potentially contradictory short, medium and long term plans.

The Short Term

The *short* term plan will need to specify objectives for the first year to two years of an incoming government, including:

- exchange control provisions, possibly based on a requirement for firms to maintain the same overall ratio in their payments as over a given time period, subject to penalties for non-compliance;
- trade control requirements on the same basis, with ceilings for imports at given previous levels, probably with a combination of tariff and quota arrangements;
- reflation of public spending (estimated to create up to ten times as many jobs as tax cuts), covered by more effective corporation tax on a standard basis plus oil revenue;
- aggregate price control levels, scheduled as rate of increase ceilings, as employed by various West European countries.

The Medium Term

The *medium* term plan for five years should roll forward annually, rather than be rigidly set for five years in advance, and should include:

- more selective exchange control procedures, including monitoring of transfer payments by multinational companies in industry and finance through the Planning Agreements procedure;
- more selective trade controls, relaxing requirements for some sectors while increasing stringency for others, also with a big business or mesoeconomic dimension introduced through Planning Agreements;
- more selective public spending allocation, including the shift towards 'social income' for those on reduced working hours or weeks, plus introduction of more specific regional redistribution of resources;
- more selective price controls, with varying degrees of stringency and relaxation, especially for price-leaders or price-makers in the big business sector.

The Long Term

The *long* terms plan should relate forecasts of feasible change beyond the rolling five year horion of the medium term plan and include:

- perspective forecasts for individual sectors, i.e. the structural dimension of economic change, with options and alternative scenarios depending on the rate of investment and innovation;
- perspective forecasts for the social distribution of such change, with employment and social income implications;
- similar perspectives for the regional and urban (i.e. spatial) distribution of such change, including its relation to the physical environment, transport etc.

A key feature of all such planning time horizons clearly should be the fullest possible involvement of trade unions at all relevant levels. The tri-partite framework of the NEDCs and SWPs should be extended to the bargaining of, not only corporate plans in the big business sector through Planning Agreements, but also the short, medium and long term planning priorities and perspectives.

Similarly, the wider public, as well as parliament, should be involved as fully as possible in the new planning horizons. They amount to a new project for the economy and society, and should be presented and debated/contested as such. For instance, at the big business level, the Planning Agreements for rail transport and power in France are part of widespread public discussion on television and radio, as well as in parliament. Such wider involvement, as well as the involvement of consumer representation and other groups, with published Social Audits of big business plans and Economic Audits by sectors and regions would be a precondition of mobilising effective support against the predictable pressures against such change.

Feasibility

Such wide-ranging new prospects for public enterprise and planning have been criticised as unfeasible by some of our own party. We have to answer this as follows.

The first response is to put quite simply: what is their own policy? It has been said that we need alternatives to Tory monetarism. On this, as against the Holy Inquisition, we can all agree. But we also need alternatives to Labour monetarism of the kind which, last time round, took some £8 billions from projected public spending and reduced real wages by ten per cent in the three years 1975-78. Lip service by latter-day converts to the Alternative Economic Strategy is sheer deception if the means to such strategic ends are denied.

The second response is to stress the essentials of the new case for public enterprise and economic planning. This lies in the fact that the market itself has massively concentrated economic power in Britain today. Just over a hundred companies now literally command two-thirds of our economy: i.e. most of activity is dominated by less than one per cent of the firms in Britain. Central government not only can, but also should, be able to account for the behaviour of such companies and also hold them to account.

The third response is that such accountability cannot be simply to government itself. The claim of corporatism would be valid if government and enterprise alone worked out the future shape of the economy. Accountability must include those who work in big and small business alike. In big business, whether public or private, the Planning Agreements system must include the right to know the forward corporate plan for the workforce, and also — critically — the right to challenge and change what such enterprise plans to do.

The fourth response is that leverage through new public ownership and public spending can give us real control over the economy and the basis of a new economic democracy. Some managers in some big business are private enterprise fanatics. Most managers want sales, market security and the gains for efficiency which go with planning. They are not only prepared to work in public enterprise but also change jobs between the private and public sectors when and where they can. Further, where public spending — as in Britain today — now represents some half of total spending, virtually no private multinational enterprise can afford to blackmail the government by foregoing its sales to the public sector.

The fifth response relates to the claim that we do not have the people to manage or plan the economy in the manner anticipated in the Alternative Economic Strategy. The argument is misconceived. It is not Labour policy that civil servants or technocrats should run British industry. Planning Agreements, as the main instrument of economic planning in the big league sector, would need to be serviced by a civil service secretariat. But the skill and expertise in such planning from the company level would and should come from those who work in the companies, and especially from white and blue collar trade unionists. For the real resource of British industry is not management alone, and certainly not industrial civil servants, but labour itself. If the Labour Party cannot give British workers a genuinely new deal in economic democracy, and carry credibility on this, then it will fall victim to Tory myths and fail as an alternative Tory party.

CHAPTER NINE

The Alternative — can it work?
Michael Meacher

We're all alternative economic strategists now, since even Denis Healey has declared his support. But that rather prompts the obvious question — *which* alternative economic strategy. What exactly is the Alternative Economic Strategy? What can it be expected to achieve? And even more importantly, what are the limits of what can be expected of it (as at present envisaged)? What are the gaps? What parts of it need to be further developed if it is to achieve the objectives intended from it?

1. THE OUTLINE OF THE ALTERNATIVE STRATEGY

The central thrust of the Alternative Economic Strategy in its original conception — and it has become even more urgent today — was the restoration of full employment, or at the very least, a massive and sustained job expansion programme leading back down the road towards full employment. The key premise for this objective was that it could be brought about if, and only if, a steady and *sustained* expansion of the economy could be realised. No other means, however necessary or desirable they might be *in addition,* would be adequate to have a decisive impact on unemployment levels reaching by 1983-4, one might extrapolate, around 3½ million.

The next question therefore is: How can a sustained economic expansion be achieved? Previously at the expansion stage of all previous trade cycles since the last war, growth has been choked off for one or other of two reasons. The first, which applied in the late 1950s and throughout the 1960s, was the import surge resulting from a high marginal propensity to import, leading to a balance of payments crisis which was then remedied by savagely deflating the home economy. The other reason, which became increasingly dominant as the main inhibitor of growth policies in the 1970s, was the fear that any Keynesian type reflation of the economy would be excessively and unacceptably inflationary. Any proposal for sustained expansion of the UK economy therefore, will have to meet these two objections.

(i) *Trade planning*

The answer of the Alternative Economic Strategy to the first objection is the imposition of import growth restraints. That these are still necessary, despite the superficially satisfactory balance of payments position of the last two years, derives from three considerations — that in many industrial sectors something over half of incremental expenditure is now used to buy imports, that the deficit for other than a highly depressed economy would now be in excess of £10 billion were it not for North Sea Oil, and that the only reason for the present trade balance is the decline in imports brought about by a huge fall in domestic demand.

What is proposed therefore is to hold the rate of growth of finished and semi-finished manufactured imports in line with the growth of exports. The domestic economy would be reflated by normal Keynesian demand management techniques, a mix of tax cuts and public expenditure increases, with a preference for the latter on the grounds that economic simulations show the latter as having a job creating capacity, for a given cost, some six times greater than the former. There would not, however, be any constraints on the growth of imports of food, fuels or raw materials, which are the staple export of the developing countries.

This mechanism would *ipso facto* secure its object of preventing a widening import gap or balance of payments crisis. But three major objections are traditionally raised against this course. Firstly, it is claimed it would lead to retaliation from exporting countries overseas, which would negate all the domestic benefits of restricting imports. This objection, however, is almost certainly greatly exaggerated. Far from any cutbacks of imports being planned, there will be a significant *increase* in import levels over and above the present level, because at the present time the most powerful import control of all is operating, namely, soaring unemployment and deep slump. All that is proposed is that the *rate of growth* of imports is held down below the level which an unfettered market exchange would otherwise produce, in order to ensure that the bulk of the extra demand generated by reflation is fed into British companies and British jobs and not into imports. But the latter would still gain rather than lose, and on that basis international complaints would be more theoretical than substantial. They would carry neither the weight nor the determination to block the Alternative Economic Strategy.

Secondly, there is, it is said, a Common Market problem. It is true that Article 30 of the Treaty of Rome prohibits any quantitative restrictions on trade between Member States. However, quite apart from the fact that the Labour Party has now clearly determined to leave the Common Market and has written this policy into its provisional Manifesto, the real issue is: Which should prevail? Should Common Market obligations override *irrespective of consequences,* even if the Alternative Economic Strategy now offered the sole remaining route available for achieving sustained growth for the U.K. economy? If this latter premise were accepted — and that is the crucial point — it is difficult to see how it would not be incumbent, let alone permissible, on a British Government to implement such a strategy at almost any cost. Certainly, the Common Market never stopped the French insisting on whatever they regarded as their overriding national interest. Nor should it stop us.

The third objection is that restraints on trade as envisaged, would featherbed industry and entrench restrictive practices still further. However, virtually all historical economic experience indicates that, if anything, the reverse is true — that high productivity is associated with rapid growth and low productivity with stagnation. If import growth restraints were an initiator of steady growth, they should herald a period of higher, rather than lower, productivity, whatever blockages or go-slows may exist for specific local reasons in particular sectors.

There are, therefore, no overriding objections at all against a policy of import growth restraints as a necessary condition for achieving steady and sustained growth. Nevertheless, whilst they may represent a necessary condition for this end, they certainly do not constitute a sufficient condition. Indeed, trade restraints are the *less important* part of the Alternative Economic Strategy. The more important part lies in the innovations in domestic industrial strategy. Whilst import planning by itself cannot be a panacea, and can only offer a breathing space, the real hinge of the policy lies in planning agreements which occupy a central role in carrying through a policy of sustained growth.

(ii) *Planning growth*

How is a steady growth performance — say 3% per year (marginally better than the 2¾% long-term annual average for the British economy) — to be secured? How can an industrial response be ensured on the supply side of the economy to match the level of the

Government's expansion on the demand side? This has been a critical unresolved problem for every Government since the War. Planning agreements uniquely offer an answer.

Despite the conventional view, a planning agreement is not so much an agreement between the boardroom of a large company and the corporate planning division of the Department of Industry about ways in which each can mutually contribute to the economy (though that is an element of what it is). It is rather a basis for joint control between management and trade unions on all the main issues which are now the unilateral prerogative of management to decide — decisions on investment, production matters, manpower planning, product development, buying and selling of industrial assets, and so on. For without trade union or shop floor consent to these specific objectives, so-called agreements between boardroom directors and top Whitehall civil servants are scarcely worth the paper they're written on.

What all this envisages is an iterative process. The overall macro-economic objectives for the economy would be set by the Government in consultation with both employer and trade union leaders (the Neddy forum, but more directional, and less a talking shop), but the essence of the new strategy would be in ensuring that the implications of these central targets carry at company level, where the real decisions affecting production are made. It would be necessary for management, having prepared the options available to corporate strategy in the light of the fullest data to hand, then to present their proposals to trade union/shop floor representatives, together with all information relevant to decisions to be made and the options entailed. The worker representatives would then determine how far they accepted these proposals, what modifications they required, and what their final negotiating position was on each specific aspect of the corporate plan. It would then be for management and worker representatives to try to reach an agreed position on each point. If so, the way would be open for the company to sign a planning agreement with government. If not, the normal give-and-take and sanctions of the negotiating process would ensue until in the normal way at some stage a compromise was reached.

What all this means in essence is the extension of trade union negotiation to all areas of decision-making in corporate strategy at present outside the scope of collective bargaining. It represents a huge enlargement of the trade union role, but it represents too an end to limiting trade union involvement to the negative use of strike power. As such, there is a real risk that the whole concept falls foul of outright opposition from *both* sides — from the management

side because it erodes their current unilateral prerogatives and from
the union side because it challenges the easier, negative role of sheer
opposition in institutionalised trench warfare in industry.

Despite these very real difficulties of making such a system work,
the planning agreements concept offers two priceless advantages,
once it has been introduced (within, say, a 3-year period) over a
wide spectrum of manufacturing industry. One is that it ensures
what has never before been possible, that key macro-economic
targets are fed into industry at the critical decision making point —
at company level from boardroom down to shop floor — to secure
a real prospect of implementation. Neither high-level tripartite
committees nor NEDO sectoral planning have previously got near
this breakthrough. Secondly, it implies a huge enlargement of the
role of trade unions. It represents an end to confining union involvement simply to the negative use of strike power. For it extends
trade union negotiation, and as a result secures union commitment
to all areas of decision making now outside the scope of collective
bargaining.

(iii) *Countering inflation*

An equally essential part of the strategy concerns how sustainable
growth can be achieved without generating excessive and in-
tolerable inflation. Now *pace* Thatcher, there are many causes of
inflation, but a primary one in the situation of countering a slump,
which is the situation the next Labour Government will face, relates
to the breakdown of Keynesian demand management. The fact is
that when governments, at least since the mid-1960s, have
stimulated the economy with extra demand, companies have not
responded by expanding production by anywhere near the same
degree — not unreasonably when Britain's high marginal propensity to import means that so much of the extra consumer expenditure
will go on imports and when regular experience of previous stop-go
cycles has indicated that an expansion surge is invariably followed
within 18-24 months by application of the brakes and another
sharp bout of deflation. It is this gap between the increase in money
in the pocket and the little or no increase in production which is
filled by inflation.

Now the Alternative Economic Strategy uniquely offers a relevant and specific answer to this problem. For one role of planning
agreements is precisely to secure a co-ordinated expansion on the
supply production side of the economy to match expansion on the
demand side applying conventional Keynesian techniques. The key
emphasis here is on *co-ordination* of the supply response. For

previously large companies, the pace-setters of the economy, have been unwilling to expand production to match the government's expansion of demand precisely because there was no guarantee their suppliers would do the same, in which case they would be hamstrung by bottlenecks, nor that their customers would do the same, in which case they would be saddled with substantial unsold stocks. Thus, it is the *systematisation* of these negotiated agreements among leading companies across the whole economy that enables companies to expand when it would otherwise be too risky to expand in isolation.

Planning agreements therefore offer a remedy never previously available for countering inflation, at least of the demand-pull kind. They thus, for the first time, open up the prospect of achieving sustainable growth without the crushing drawback of unacceptably high inflation. That alone is a measure of the importance of the Alternative Economic Strategy.

2. A CRITIQUE OF THE ALTERNATIVE ECONOMIC STRATEGY

But having outlined some of the key elements of the Alternative Economic Strategy, it is essential, if we are to recognise weaknesses and gaps that certainly still exist, to subject the whole system to critical analysis whilst there is still time to make the necessary remedies. I believe there are at least five areas which require such scrutiny.

(a) *How many new jobs will it actually create?*

What is still not yet widely realised is the sheer enormity of the job-creating task the Alternative Economic Strategy faces. Department of Employment data shows that no less than 40% of those taking up new jobs in an expansionary phase are those who were not previously registered as unemployed, chiefly married women. This means that the current total of those effectively in the labour market but without jobs is not, in accordance with the present unemployment rate (August 1981) 2.9 million, but some 4.7 million. Given that, at least a further three-quarters of a million must be expected to be made redundant under current Tory policies before the next election, and given too that demographically the number of persons of working age is expected to rise by another three quarters of a million over the next 5 years, *at least 5 million jobs* require to be created before this country can return to anything like full employment. Can the Alternative Economic Strategy produce even remotely a jobs total like that?

Perhaps the maximum that can be expected would be made up as follows. A devaluation of sterling by 35% would, according to model simulations recently published by Cambridge Econometrics, generate one million jobs — provided that other countries did not negate some of the UK gain by counter-devaluations, and provided the unions and professional and managerial associations accept a firm policy on incomes to prevent the huge job creating potential being swept away by spiralling pay claims to enhance real living standards. Once the devaluation has had maximum effect on jobs from export expansion, say after 18-24 months, a series of modest but continuing reflationary packages should be launched, perhaps in the range of £3-5 billion annually, together with some control over the growth of imports to ensure the benefits are largely concentrated on British jobs and British products and not on imports. Two qualifications are needed here. One is that to launch domestic reflation at an earlier stage would risk diverting the export drive into satisfying home demand, and would thus sacrifice the jobs to be derived from the former. Secondly, restraint on the *growth* of imports (no cutback) should be by quota — say 2-5% per year — rather than by tariff surcharge, since, as Cambridge Econometrics has shown, the job-creating potential of the former is much greater than that of the latter (unless raised by unrealistic amounts of 50% or more). Subject to these qualifications, three such reflationary packages in the latter half of a 5-year Parliamentary term should generate 1½ million extra jobs.

In addition to this main thrust of macro-economic strategy, two other complementary measures might create a further half to one million jobs. One would be the banning of overtime. If this were achieved completely and all the work redistributed to create new jobs, an extra 1.3 million jobs would result, it has been estimated. Bearing in mind, however, the inevitable mismatch between the availability of extra work and suitable workers (let alone the thorny political problems of gaining worker consent) a more realistic figure here might be an extra half to three-quarters of a million jobs. Secondly, a major boost should be given to the Co-operative Development Agency to promote industrial co-operatives and small-scale labour-intensive enterprise on the substantial scale that could clearly be viable, and also to Local Enterprise Boards developing job opportunities in the main cities throughout the country. That could produce an additional half million jobs over a 5-year period.

With these last two initiatives included, the aggregate of new jobs that might be generated by all these measures totals some 3-3½ million. It is still some way short of the 5 million required, but if

achieved, would represent the biggest onslaught on unemployment
in any Western country since the war.

(b) *Would it be intolerably inflationary?*

How can the inflationary potential of both a major devaluation
and successive domestic reflations be contained? For estimates by
economists David Blake and Paul Ormerod, based on re-working
the Treasury model, indicate that both these routes to expansion
entail heavy inflationary costs. One of their simulations involved
devaluation of the £ by 20%, which they found increased employment by 400,000 and output by 5%, but at the same time raised inflation to 19% (from 12%), followed by a gradual fall to 14% in
three years, by which time living standards would have declined by
3%. Another simulation envisaged a £6 billion reflation plus a 30%
rise in tariffs on manufactures, which was shown to produce an extra 600,000 jobs, but at the expense of an increase in inflation to
20%. How then, can these undesirable side-effects be avoided, or
at least minimised, so that the whole strategy is not swept away in a
surge of inflation?

It is likely that implementation of the Alternative Economic
Strategy will release both demand-pull *and* cost-push inflation,
because a massive expansion of demand is a key part of the strategy
and because once monetarism is overturned and the Tories
defeated, it is all too likely that it will be interpreted by the unions
and other pay negotiators that the brakes are finally off. Both types
of inflation will, therefore, need to be met.

It has already been indicated that the demand-pull form of inflation can be effectively, and uniquely, met within the Alternative
Economic Strategy via the role of planning agreements as complementing traditional Keynesian demand management with
management of the supply side of the economy. Provided the level
of demand is not boosted too sharply, too fast, planning
agreements for the first time do offer a means for the government
to regulate the production/investment response so that the
demand-supply balance in the economy does not get markedly out
of kilter.

Meeting the challenge of cost-push inflation requires different
measures. The central question here, which must be clearly asked
and clearly answered, is whether there is any way by which the
government can at the same time increase investment (public as well
as private), increase public expenditure (to remedy the cuts), and
increase social benefits (to redress the real fall in living standards of
social service beneficiaries), all of which is required under the

Alternative Economic Strategy — *and* enhance post-tax real incomes as well. If the honest answer to this is that there is no way, what can be the basis for regulating a pay explosion?

One reply consistent with the Alternative Economic Strategy is that the counterpart to the planning of production, investment and trade is the planning of incomes. What would otherwise be a constraint on trade union power, in an in other respects capitalist free-for-all, can fit naturally into a genuinely socialist planning framework so long as (i) all the other key elements in the economy are equally subject to planned control, and (ii) the planning is directly participated in by the workers' representatives themselves and not paternatistically thrust on them from above. That is one answer, that an agreed policy for some limitation on incomes is not by any means a rhetorical cover for naked wage restraint, but a reflection on the impossibility otherwise of meeting other economic targets equally demanded by unions and workers, and a limited concession anyway compensated by a very real *quid pro quo,* both in political and monetary terms. In power terms there is a trade-off in access via planning agreements to all key industrial decision making at company and local level. But since monetary sacrifice today, no doubt in the last analysis, will only stick if balanced by increased monetary gain tomorrow, perhaps either a proportion of income tax could be repaid by government as index linked savings after (say) 3 years according to the degree of pay restraint or, perhaps better, once planning agreements were in place, limitation on pay could be exchanged for the right to share in the firm's consequentially increased capital appreciation. Such details are, of course, matters for negotiation, but there can be little doubt that some such balanced trade-off, entirely consistent with a socialist redistribution of power and wealth to workers, will be necessary.

(c) *What role for planning agreements?*

Another issue which needs to be faced is whether planning agreements, at the heart of the Alternative Economic Strategy , can actually fulfill the roles that are thrust upon them according to different dimensions of the strategy. At least quite separate roles can be disentangled. One is to achieve a form of industrial democracy of much more direct application than that presented by the Bullock formula. Another, as already described, is to supplement conventional Keynesian demand management with the means for supply management. And a third is to offer a device for regulating the multinationals and other big comanies. Given that each of these roles might be viable by itself, are they all compatible with a single planning instrument?

Planning agreements are indeed being expected to perform some very different functions — to decentralise industrial decision making so that the Alternative Economic Strategy does not degenerate into a corporatist economic strategy; to prevent a rash of demand-pull inflation that could knock the whole strategy off course; and to ensure that multinational and other big companies operate broadly in line with the Alternative Economic Strategy and don't sabotage or buck it. Yet there are difficulties with each of these roles.

On the first count, there is inevitably tension between central and decentralised planning under the Alternative Economic Strategy. Planning agreements would by themsleves be of little use outside the context of a national plan for the overall allocation of resources, and this in turn demands a very different type of civil servant. For the British civil service is at present totally opposed to the management of a dirigiste economic policy, compared, say, to the French, who have created top level industrial cadres for just this purpose. On the second count, it must be doubted whether planning agreements can be set in place quickly enough and wide-rangingly enough to attain this end. But is that an argument for making the exercise compulsory, to be operating within a reasonably short span of time (1-2 years), and to be effected with maximum trade union preparation and involvement. On the third count, it is frequently objected that the reach of planning agreements is confined to the UK, whilst multinationals are directed extra-territorially. But this is to under-rate the effectiveness of the determined imposition of planning priorities. Thus MITI successfully insists on the transfer of new technology as a condition for investment in Japan. France absolutely insists on adherence to the French planning framework, and prevents all foreign takeovers in key areas. The USA, despite all the rhetoric of free enterprise, leant heavily on BP to go into partnership with Sohio for the recovery of Alaskan oil.

In the light of all this, the conclusion must be that planning agreements have greater potential than has yet been widely recognised, but their potency will depend a great deal on the firmness and determination of those who launch the exercise.

(d) *Will import restraints breed retaliation?*

Trade planning is essential for maintaining sustained growth once the devaluation effects have worn off. But can it hold if widespread retaliation results?

It has already been argued that this scenario is unlikely when other countries will do *better* in terms of exporting to the UK than they do now in slump conditions when unemployment is far more of an inhibitor of imports than bureaucratic controls are ever likely to be. Moreover, the Third World should *gain* rather than lose under the Alternative Economic Strategy, both because there would be no limit on the growth of imports of foods, fuels or raw materials, and also because trade planning would permit a measure of positive discrimination on their behalf in respect of manufactures.

The key point here is that there are two types of import restraint, one of which is bad for world trade and one of which is virtuous. It is bad if import controls are used simply to protect the balance of payments. That *does* mean the export of unemployment, and it does represent a zero sum gain in which Britain only gains at the expense of others. But there is another kind whereby import controls, without in any way redressing any balance of payments difficulties there maybe, are simply used to raise domestic output. Because there is no cutback in imports there can be no export of unemployment, and *both* Britain *and* overseas countries would gain from an expanding UK economy. Nor would it be a danger that other countries might adopt the same course, both because the aim for Britain would not be export promotion but import substitution at the margin, and also because such a scenario would have the same beneficial effects for Britain as undertaking this policy in Britain has for them.

For these reasons, talk of trade retaliation, including, for example, citing the recent Indonesian banning of certain British industrial orders because of MFA restrictions on some of their textile exports to the UK, misses the point that trade planning under the Alternative Economic Strategy is not of this import reducing kind. Contrary to all the conventional reflexes about limitations on free trade — which should anyway scarcely distract socialists — what is recommended here is an expansionary measure which is in other countries' interest as well as ours.

(e) *What complementary controls over financial institutions?*

To bring all these industrial and economic measures to fruition, clearly a number of accompanying financial measures are also required. Firstly, there is an urgent need to re-introduce exchange controls, when in the year following abolition direct investment abroad trebled to £2,000 million at an annual rate. Secondly, for regulating investment flows overseas, there is need of a Foreign Investment Review Agency, on lines already pioneered by several other countries, which would apply DOI criteria about suitability of investment location (i.e. why the investment had to be abroad and could not be undertaken in the UK) rather than exclusively Treasury criteria about protecting the capital account on the balance of payments.

Thirdly, if a significant increase in public sector investment is to be financed, it is essential that rather than sending the PSBR through the ceiling, more direct controls should be established over the huge semi-compulsorily exacted annual revenues of the pension and insurance funds. Their total income now amounts to £10½ billion per year, and their aggregate funds to some £60 billion. Minute regard for the profit-maximizing interests of the individual policy holder, with blithe disregard for the interests of the national economy by which the welfare of all policy holders, ultimately stands or falls, is simply no longer realistic. Again, on the precedent of several other Western governments' initiatives, a proportion of pension and insurance funds' annual income (say, 30–50%) should be required to be invested in certain approved sectors of British manufacturing.

Lastly, there is the vital need to ensure that industrial expansion is adequately financed at moderate cost — which means at interest rates on medium-term loans not higher than those fixed for competitors overseas. It is true that the Wilson Committee on City Institutions found that the main stumbling block was lack of investment opportunity because of poor prospects of future demand and profitability, but once an atmosphere of sustained expansion changes this, the very high interest rate structure in Britain, particularly on medium-term facilities, could well prove prohibitive. For this purpose what is needed is a National Investment Bank, with bills rediscounted via the Bank of England, to provide loans at low interest (perhaps around 5%) for approved manufacturing investment, especially in potential growth sectors like scientific equipment, robotics, control engineering and office equipment.

In summary, it should be concluded that the Alternative Economic Strategy uniquely offers Britain an escape route to expansion and the return towards full employment away from the dead ends of the now discredited Establishment bipartisan consensus of 1951-79 and of the the disastrous monetarist collapse since 1979. The strategy still needs further elaboration, and above all it needs to be further worked over, thought through and familiarised with by the Labour movement. But, whilst it is by no means to be confused with socialism itself, it is certainly an important part of that transformation process to socialism which, for that reason alone, warrants commitment throughout the Movement.

CHAPTER TEN

Working Time:
the critical problem*

John Hughes

INTRODUCTION

An employment crisis of immense severity for working people is developing in Britain. This crisis is emerging from a combination of:

— weaknesses in economic development and performance;
— recent policies in the management of the national economy;
— and the rigidities of approach to conventional patterns of working time.

A number of serious issues of policy, for society in general, for the trade unions in particular, and for management and administration, clearly require to be resolved in the connected areas of employment and the organisation of working time.

To grasp the severity of the problem is it perhaps only necessary to emphasise what is happening to registered unemployment in the UK. Since the recession of 1975 unemployment remained persistently higher than ever before in the post war years, never falling below 1⅓ million, with a particular concentration among young workers under 25. By the spring of 1981 registered unemployment has already reached 2½ millions, or over 10% of the entire total of employees. Most forecasts expect unemployment to exceed 3 millions by 1982, and a number of serious analysts expect further substantial rises in unemployment by the mid-1980s.

But these figures do not signal adequately the exceptional crisis of *manual* work. Against a background of long term decline in the number of manual jobs in the economy, 80% of the unemployed men and nearly half the unemployed female workers are registered as from manual occupations. The number of unemployed manual workers, already at around 1⅓ million, represent a "surplus army" of 20% compared with the number of manual jobs for full-

---

*An extended version of a paper delivered to a seminar on *The Social Organisation of Time,* held in Milan in June 1981, under the auspices of the Biennale of Venice.

time workers in the economy.

To understand the connection of the general employment crisis with the existing patterns of organisation of working time, it is essential that the special features of working time in the British economy should be recognised. It is important too, to recognise the significance of important trends in work that have developed over the last decade. The debate over the future of working time has to respect the realities of working time in Britain. Yet these are not fully understood and false stereotypes still influence discussion and attitudes to policy. Concern with reality is the more evident a need since changes in working time have to be approached within constraints as to unit labour costs; weaknesses in international competitive performance and problems of financing labour-intensive public services combine to emphasise persistence of such cost constraints.

The trade unions have come forward since the late 1970s actively campaigning and bargaining for reduced working time, and have already secured some important changes. But their policies will need to develop considerably further in the face of the critical problems of the 1980s. Consequently, detailed analysis and research into the organisation of working time and into case studies of change are important to them.

SPECIAL CHARACTERISTICS OF WORKING TIME IN BRITAIN

The following elements cannot be neglected in any discussion. They include persistent features of the British organisation of working time, as well as some important trends that became particularly apparent through the 1970s:

(a) *There are significant differences in working time and its associated conditions as between manual and non-manual workers*

In the past manual work predominated, but by now the number of employees in employment across the economy as a whole is split almost equally between manual and non-manual work; however, some two-thirds of manufacturing employees are manual workers.

Until recently the "basic" weekly hours of manual workers were, typically, 40 hours, whereas non-manual basic weeks are more dispersed, but in the early 1970s centred around 37½ hours, and around only 36-37 hours in the later 1970s. Some differentiation of annual holidays persists in favour of non-manual workers (approximately one week more). Generally, non-manual workers enjoy more protection of their income in face of absence from work (in a typical week 15% of manual workers will lose some earnings due to not working a full week compared with only 5% of non-manual workers). Systems of "flexi-hours" are relatively widespread among non-manuals. Other elements of differentiation exist in conditions; differences in industrial pension provision have been reduced but are still apparent. Thus, in Britain, the question of reforming and reducing working time cannot be separated from the elements of discrimination that operate as between these two broad categories of workers.

(b) *The relative and absolute decline in* full-time *jobs for employees has characterised the last decade.*

The fall in *full-time* employees in work has contrasted with a broadly stable number of male employees (in work or registered as unemployed) and a sizeable increase in the number of female employees. My own estimates from official figures suggest that, whereas the total number of employees in Great Britain (in or out of employment) is about 1.3 million higher than a decade ago (in 1971) the number of employees *in full-time work* is around *1.3 million lower* than a decade ago. The difference is largely accounted for by unemployment increase among males, and is split between increased unemployment and increased part-time work among females. It is important to note that despite the large increase in the number of females seeking work in the British economy over the last decade (my calculation from official data suggests an increase of 1.3 million; in reality — since not all female job seekers register — it may be higher) the number in full-time jobs is marginally fewer. *Table 1, Employees in Great Britain, 1971 to 1981,* gives details.

The change in ratios, in *relative* proportions, is quite startling. It is worth remembering, in looking at the contrast involved between 1971 and 1981, that 1971 was also a year of economic depression (involving hitherto unprecedented levels of post-war unemployment in Britain). Taking the total number of employees (as 100) and splitting them into the categories of full-time employees, part-time employees and registered unemployed, offers the following contrast between 1971 and 1981:

	1971	1981
Full Time	82%	72%
Part-time	15%	18%
Unemployed	3%	10%

(Data derived from Table 1)

The separation of these changes as they affected male employees and female employees is instructive:

	Males		Females	
	1971	1981	1971	1981
Full Time	92%	83%	66%	55%
Part Time	4%	5%	33%	38%
Unemployed	4%	12%	1%	7%

The social significance of the diversion of female aspirations for wider job opportunities into part-time work and unemployment must be highly important.

(c) *There has been a marked increase in part-time employment*

The increase in part-time employment has been most notable for women workers. Part-time employment is notoriously difficult to measure, but on the consistent definition of the Census of Employment part-time employment of female employees rose by one million between 1971 and 1978 (nearly 4.4 millions).

There was considerable expansion of part-time employment in the *public* services in the first half of the 1970s, and, indeed, this acted as an offset to employment decline in the 1975 recession. But, subsequently, increasingly severe public service expenditure constraints have checked further employment growth.

The *private* services sector has been particularly important as a source of part-time employment. *Table 2, Growth of Part-time Employment,* sets out the data for the main private services. What becomes clear is that there is a distinct pattern of the *substitution* of part-time female in place of full-time workers; this is especially clear cut in the retail distributive trades where the strong rise in part-time employment, if thought of as "full-time equivalents", is an exact match for the decline in full-time female employment.

These trends have important social implications, and pose problems for the trade unions, not only because they may disappoint the job expectations of women workers, but also because of the increasing scale of the problems of inferior job status, inferior pay, conditions and career prospects, and the difficulties of trade union organisation and policy that arises from the extension of part-time employment. Still more so when the phenomenon connects with a decline in full-time employment. Looking back, the apparent achievement of "equal pay" for women workers in the 1970s contrasts awkwardly with these realities. Looking forward, it is precisely in the private service sectors characterised by such trends that we are expected to look for increased employment in the 1980s.

(d) *There is a strongly marked trend to the absolute and relative decline of manual employment in the UK economy.*

Through the 1970s an absolute fall in full-time manual employment went alongside an expansion in non-manual employment. By 1979 (prior to the current slump) full time adult manual employment had fallen to 8.4 millions compared with 10 millions in 1970. By contrast full-time adult non-manual employment rose from 7 millions in 1970 to 8 millions by 1979. *Table 3, Manual and Non-Manual Employment 1970 and 1979,* attempts an analysis of the main categories, for both the male and the female labour force. The decline in manual employment has particularly centred on manufacturing, due both to economic decline and technological change; this point is commented on subsequently.

Consistently, the South-Eastern region of England has had a much higher proportion of non-manual employment than other regions. This means that the long period decline in manual employment is developing into increasingly serious "structural" problems of unemployment in other regions of the economy, particularly for manual men, and for young workers with limited educational qualifications.

(e) *There has been a high incidence of overtime working among manual men*

Some discussions of overtime working in Britain fail to emphasise sufficiently strongly that high levels of overtime working are particularly concentrated among manual men. As *Table 3* shows, manual men by 1979 accounted for only 30% of the total number of employees in employment (compared with over 36% in 1970). Before the current economic slump nearly 60% of manual men worked overtime in any given week, and those who did so averaged over 10 hours overtime, so that one should think of an average 50-hour "actual" working week for such workers. These levels of overtime working showed little year to year variation. The overall pattern of overtime working, and the contrast with women workers and non-manual men, is set out in *Table 4, Overtime and Shiftwork: Full-time Adult Employees.*

There has been a strong tendency for industries with relatively high overtime hours worked by manual men to have relatively low basic hourly wages. (In 1979 the twelve manufacturing industries with the highest levels of average overtime included seven with hourly earnings considerably below the manufacturing average, two below, and three close to the average. Outside manufacturing, transport and communication industries are characterised by high overtime; in the main industries involved hourly earnings are considerably lower than in manufacturing). On average, for the manual men working overtime in any week, overtime pay constitutes nearly a quarter of total earnings.

In a typical week before the current slump, around 5 million workers would be working overtime (4 million of those being manual men) compared to around 12 million other full-time workers not doing so. If one were to think of aggregated overtime hours in equivalents of "normal" full-time jobs, then the overtime of manual men produces an equivalent of around one million jobs. But for all full-time women workers the figure would be very small, around 80,000 job equivalents, and for non-manual men some 175,000 job equivalents.

(f) *There is an associated problem of long hours of shiftworkers*

Shiftworking in the British economy has been compensated for by the development of premium payments rather than by reduced hours. (The only qualification to that is that under many agreements shift workers have a half-hour paid meal break within the shift whereas 'day' workers have not). *Table 4* shows the incidence of shiftwork, and the scale of the premia paid. But it also shows that there exists a major problem of long hours among manual men, and the average overtime worked by shiftworkers was, at the survey date, higher than for that of all categories of workers. It would appear that shiftworking teams have not been reorganised in recent years to reflect shorter basic hours (not even, necessarily, the reduction to 40 hours in the late 1960s) nor longer annual holidays, and in consequence high levels of overtime are widespread among shiftworkers. Shift work is mainly found in capital intensive manufacturing industries, and in certain public services (notably transport and hospitals). Hospitals account for the biggest grouping of shiftworkers among non-manual categories. Nurses' hours have been particularly onerous (the nominal 40-hour "basic" week not shortened by any paid meal breaks, but lengthened by meal breaks and the time taken to prepare for work); they are still in actual practice comparatively high despite the very recent (April 1981) reduction of the basic week to 37½ hours. It is significant that in almost all cases the recent reduction in nurses' basic hours has been handled by a 2½-hour block reduction in one day, or (for night workers) by building up additional paid leave days. (Case studies have generally shown workers' preferences in the organisation of shorter working time for the creation of a useful block of additional leisure time).

(g) *There is a special problem of job displacement and of un-balanced working time in manufacturing industries.*

Both the decline in full time employment and the rapid fall in manual employment are intimately connected with the un-precedented secular decline of British manufacturing industries over the last decade. Despite only sluggish improvements in labour productivity (associated with low investment and under-capacity working) total employment in manufacturing has fallen by two millions since 1970. As nearly 70% of employment in manufactur-ing is still manual in character this fall has been particularly con-centrated on manual workers. Official estimates show the total "in-put" of hours worked by "operatives" (i.e. manual workers) in manufacturing to have fallen by 35% in the last decade; the fall is continuing at a rapid pace. If average weekly hours per operative had not also fallen, by an officially estimated 10%, the impact on employment would have been even more severe.

As it is, the current crisis in British manufcturing provided an astonishing spectacle of the disintegration of full-time employment and of the uneven distribution of the work that is available. My estimate is that there are currently some 4.8 million manual workers employed in manufacturing industry or unemployed but with manufacturing as their last job. The distribution of their working time is as follows:

Manual Workers in Manufacturing: Spring 1981
(Rounded estimates)

Unemployed	500,000
Part-time	300,000
Short time	600,000 (av. loss of 14 hours per week)
Normal hours, full-time	2,400,000
Overtime worked, full-time	1,000,000 (av. 8 hours overtime)

(Sources: Estimates from official data including Table 1.11 of the *Employment Gazette*).

It is perhaps a mathematical accident that if the normal working week were 35 hours and no overtime was worked, there would be the equivalent of full-time work for 4½ million operatives and part-time for the present 300,000; this would exactly match the cur-rent total of workers including those unemployed and on short time.

THE "DEBATE" AND DEVELOPMENTS SO FAR

Since the debate began in earnest in 1977/78 there has been strong resistance to trade union pressure for reductions in working time from both governments and employers. The main arguments used have been that the shorter "basic" week would lead on a large scale into overtime*, that this would amplify the rise in unit labour costs (from shortening hours without loss of pay), and that this in turn would worsen comparative costs and damage competitiveness. It has also been suggested that these problems would be intensified by shortages of skilled labour in "segmented" labour markets.

The trade unions in 1978, through the TUC, argued the possibility of associating the shortening of the working week with efficiency bargaining. The Labour Government replied by adding to its incomes policy White Paper ("Winning The Battle Against Inflation", July 1978) the grudging concession that shorter basic hours could be considered but only if they were costless:

> "The Government can accept a reduction in hours as part of a normal pay settlement on condition that it is demonstrated that the settlement as a whole does not lead to any increase in unit costs above what would have resulted from a straight guideline settlement on pay . . . Indeed, the cost of any improvement in conditions of employment such as holidays, hours . . . must count towards the level of settlements save insofar as any cost involved is fully offset by increased productivity".

The Trade Union Research Unit, in its analysis and from its case studies, has throughout considered that an efficiency bargaining approach, within a wider "social contract" concerned with reducing unemployment, could be a particularly beneficial collective bargaining approach. (Earlier "productivity bargaining" in the 1960s had generally "traded off" increased productivity and reduced manning against higher earnings and bonuses rather than against significantly reduced basic and actual working time). Detailed bargaining about resource use in direct association with shorter working time could combine the real benefit to existing workers from increased leisure with improved capital and labour

---

*The official *Employment Gazette,* in April 1978, carried an article on work-sharing (p.400), which incorrectly exaggerated the extent to which earlier (mid-1960s) reductions in the basic week had led into increased overtime. But in other estimates, in fact, in response to Trade Union Research Unit analysis on shorter hours, it did show that shortening the basic week would bring substantial benefit to the balance of public finances. (The original TURU analysis of the 35-hour week in Britain appeared in the DGB's *WSI Mitteilungen,* September 1977, and in *Full Employment, Priority,* publishers Spokesman, Gamble Street, Nottingham, in my name. See also for the criticism of *Employment Gazette* and CBI arguments, John Hughes' *A Shorter Working Week,* IWC Pamphlet No. 63, Bertrand Russell House, Gamble Street, Nottingham.

productivity, and scope for employment creation. As official studies had suggested that shortening the basic week under such conditions would benefit public finances, it would have been rational for government policy to be more supportive.

The first major *collective bargaining* breakthrough was, interestingly, in this style and notionally paid some respect to the Government's White Paper policy. In practice it was only because of long sustained industrial action through 1978 that the Post Office Engineers (over a hundred thousand strong) won the 37½-hour week. Rank and file pressure here stemmed from deep concern as to the long run implications of new technology for employment prospects, but also reflected reaction to the shorter working time of non-manual engineers (supervisors, high technicians, etc.). The arbitration settlement provided for efficiency bargaining, and this at regional level included interesting changes in shift duration (including for many workers longer shift times, but a nine-day fortnight).

In 1979 the area of collective bargaining pressure widened dramatically, notably with a lengthy and extremely damaging engineering dispute in the autumn which finally wrenched the concession of a 39-hour week (from 1981) from bitterly reluctant employers. Many other agreements followed, those pressing for an early and major reduction of weekly hours having often to resort to strike action (e.g. printing). The general outcome has been widespread reduction in basic manual hours to 39, or to 37½ hours over a phased period (in chemicals till 1985); widespread but still minor lengthening of holiday entitlements; and through a comparability study the reduction in the basic week of nurses (nearly half a million affected) from 40 to 37½ hours.

A very recent analysis in the *Employment Gazette* for April 1981 ("Recent Changes in Hours and Holiday Entitlements") covers only manual workers and their agreements. It shows just under half a million workers affected by reduced basic hours in 1980, but estimates that "at least 3.2 million workers" will have a reduction in hours in 1981. During 1980 agreements covering 3½ million workers provided for increases in holiday entitlements. Already, by 1980, 74% of manual workers had basic holidays of four weeks and over, compared with only 35% in 1978. An estimated further three million workers will become entitled to extra paid holidays in 1981. No equivalent official estimates covering non-manual workers have appeared.

It is probably true that the impact of the movement so far has been limited by the intensity of the economic depression in 1980-81 and the shift of bargaining emphasis to defensiveness and concern with redundancy; the recession has also led to widespread temporary work sharing through short time working (with income support from a governmental scheme). Otherwise, more "efficiency" bargaining around reductions in working time might have accompanied more sizeable reductions in basic working time. Instead, many employers have taken advantage of their power in a period of intense economic depression to push through demanning and reorganisation of working practices in a unilateral way. We should recognise that there have been, in this sense, retreats, as well as advances..

However, given the harsh economic climate, the impact that trade union bargaining pressure has had in reducing working time is impressive. The TUC's own assessment (TUC Consultative Document: "Unemployment and Working Time", Feb. 1981) is that:

> "Two of the greatest barriers to shorting working time — the 40 hour week for manual workers and the 4-week basic holiday entitlement — have now been comprehensively breached".

The TUC goes on to lay major emphasis in its report on the importance of drastically reducing overtime working. Unusually for the British trade union movement, it openly discusses the need for legislation to curb overtime, and indicates that just over half the trade unions that responded to its questions on this issue were prepared to see legislation used. The operation of overtime is, in practice, deeply rooted in many industries' systems of work organisation and in employers' response to the labour market. Overtime is not a matter that can be dealt with on its own in isolation from other issues of pay and conditions; for instance major reductions in overtime for manual men would raise questions of shift work teams and manning, low basic pay, recruitment and retention of skilled workers, and the use of overtime as an element in local bargaining at plant level.

An associated matter is that of protective legislation on hours, shift work and overtime, dating from the nineteenth century and aimed at protecting women workers and juveniles. It is currently being argued by the Equal Opportunities Commission (in a report, "Health and Safety Legislation: Should we distinguish between men and women?") that this may represent discrimination against women.* The trade union movement's response has been to suggest

---

*For a criticism, see Discussion Paper No.23, *The Control of Working Hours and Health and Safety Legislation,* the Trade Union Research Unit, Ruskin College, Oxford.

that such legislation needs re-working to apply to both men and women. This could be an important element in future policy discussions, and offer a route to closer control over both overtime and shiftworking arrangements.

SOME ISSUES OF THE FUTURE ORGANISATION OF WORKING TIME

It is clear from the preceding analysis that, as yet, both the discussion of working time in Britain and the pressures of the trade unions through collective bargaining have only just begun to challenge the country's traditional patterns of working time. They have only begun, too, to recognise and react to the trends that have become apparent in recent years, and which have been replacing full-time work with part-time employment and with structural unemployment.

As a small example of the new responses of trade unions to this situation we may take the recent annual conference of USDAW (Union of Shop, Distributive and Allied Workers, with half a million members). This adopted a policy document stating that Union negotiators in retail trade should seek undertakings that future employment (full- or part-time) will be given to workers who are not in any other employment, thus attempting to attack "moonlighting" and the casual employment of workers already in full-time employment. The emphasis is explicitly a work sharing one.

The research studies of the Trade Union Research Unit have revealed a preference on the part of workers for the shortening of working time to take the form of meaningful gains in access to blocks of leisure time (rather than marginal reductions in daily shift time). This suggests that the shorter working week may be arrived at within the framework of eight-hour shifts (or, indeed, longer ones as, with the post office engineers), but with re-organisation of working time to provide longer weekends freed from work, or nine-day fortnights or four-day weeks, or additional rest days. This could be an important means of challenging old patterns of working time, including excessive overtime, especially if agreements provide for additional time off in lieu of overtime that is worked.

The new readiness of the TUC to challenge extensive overtime working should be seen in this context and raises wider issues of social policy and economic organisation. We have already cited the unresolved issue of the reform of earlier laws protecting women workers in certain industries so far as shiftwork and overtime are concerned. It is almost certainly true that the major advances recently secured in longer annual holidays could leak into overtime working (to cover for workers absent on holiday) unless trade unions take a much more systematic approach to the use of collective bargaining to control the necessary recruitment and increased manning required. The existing structure of employment taxation falling on employers (notably the National Insurance levies) has encouraged employers to limit recruitment and extend overtime working (which is not penalised through taxation and other on-costs to any equivalent extent).

But the social debate, and trade union responses, must extend much further to review the needs of less well protected workers, notably the unemployed, and those experiencing the inferior status and security of part-time work. It is because there are genuine cost constraints that might check policies aimed at increased employment, that collective bargaining priorities may need to be redirected towards a conscious pursuit of increased employment opportunities. It is ironic that governments which have resisted reduction of working time (on the grounds that it might worsen comparative labour costs) have at the same time pursued or tolerated policies raising the sterling exchange rate in recent years so that a major deterioration of comparative costs has, in fact, occurred. But that does not make the problems associated with rising unit labour costs any less real. The same may be said for the financing problems associated with the maintenance and extension of labour-intensive public services. This invites not only a collective bargaining style concerned with both efficiency and employment creation; it suggests the need for a future government to give priority to a fairer distribution of work opportunities in broad alliance with trade union concerns to raise employment.

One possibility that should not be neglected would be the development of a more flexible, but bargained and planned, interpretation of full-time work. Instead of the full-time work week being defined as one specific set of hours, there might be a range of hours (say 32 to 38) that might carry the status and rights and conditions of full time work. Older workers, and many women workers, might opt for the lower end of the range of such work weeks, whereas at present, industrial discipline requires the full specified hours to be worked.

Moreover, in Britain, we are only beginning to recognise the need for a better balanced transition from school to work, with a planned programme of education, training and work experience supplementing the working time of young workers. The TUC has persistently supported the Manpower Services Commission in its efforts to secure additional funding for programmes that can attack youth unemployment. But it is increasingly clear that this requires a major re-appraisal of the balance of working time and of other constructive educational and developmental activities of younger workers.

In much the same way, the debate in Britain is only slowly beginning to take up the question of a more human and constructive phased transition from work to eventual retirement towards the end of people's full-time working lives. This too, as with the transition for young workers, invites a balance of work, of education and adaptation for "social skills" and personal interests. Given the potential flexibility and real financial power, of industrial pension funds, it should be possible, both through collective bargaining and through more constructive intervention by the state, to organise such "transitions" in many ways that will ease the burden of work on older workers, help their personal development and adaptation, and release jobs for other workers. Socially, it may be much better to redirect part-time work towards the transition into work and from work, while limiting the extent to which employers can deploy part-time work as a substitute for full-time work across the main range of adult working life.

In between these two transitions there is, as yet, too limited a debate about the scope for paid educational leave, and its role in the socially complex and technologically advancing society of the future. Our educational institutions in Britain are, instead, trapped in defensive struggles for diminishing financial resources as the government develops successive — and increasingly arbitrary — cuts in real levels of spending across all parts of the educational system. Meanwhile, the current crisis of employment and unemployment unfolds with devastating speed and scope.

Table 1: Employees in Great Britain, 1971 to 1981
(in thousands)

MALES	June 1971	June 1978	June 1980	February 1981
In Employment (total) of which	13,424	13,096	12,831	(12,350)
Full-time	12,840	12,392	(12,151)	(11,700)
Part-time	584	704	(680)	(650)
Unemployed	589	978	1,083	1,686
All Male Employees	14,013	14,074	13,914	(14,036)

FEMALES

In employment (total)	8,224	9,158	9,178	(8,950)
of which				
Full-time	5,468	5,478	5,413	(5,300)
Part-time	2,757	3,679	3,765	(3,650)
Unemployed	98	403	504	677
All Female Employees	8,332	9,561	9,682	(9,627)

MALES AND FEMALES

In employment (total)	21,648	22,253	22,008	(21,300)
of which				
Full-time	18,307	17,870	(17,564)	(17,000)
Part-time	3,341	4,384	(4,444)	(4,300)
Unemployed	687	1,381	1,587	2,363
ALL EMPLOYEES	22,335	23,634	23,595	(23,663)

Sources: Census of Employment for 1971; official estimates for June 1980; Registered Unemployment data. *Author's estimates are bracketed.*

Table 2: Growth of Part-time Female Employment in Retail Distribution, Financial and Miscellaneous Services
(thousands)

	1971	1977	Change 1971 – 77 (000s)	As %
Full-time				
Retail Distribution	633.3	560.7	— 72.6	—11%
Insurance, Financial Serv.	365.9	406.6	+ 40.7	+11%
Miscellaneous Services	548.6	562.9	+ 14.3	+ 3%
Part-time				
Retail Distribution	534.6	673.6	+139.0	+ 26%
Insurance, Financial Serv.	123.8	176.7	+ 52.9	+43%
Miscellaneous Services	482.7	755.6	+272.9	+57%

Source: Census of Employment.

Table 3: Manual and Non-Manual Employment, 1970 and 1979
(Great Britain, Millions)

	Manual		Non-Manual	
	1970	1979	1970	1979
Full-time Men	8.0	6.8	3.9	4.4
Full-time Women	2.0	1.6	3.1	3.6

Youths (Full Time)	0.9	0.8	0.3	0.3
Girls (Full-time)	0.2	0.1	0.3	0.2
Part-time Male	0.4	0.4	0.2	0.3
Part-time Female	1.7	2.0	1.0	1.8
All Full-time	11.1	9.3	7.6	8. 5
All Part-time	2.1	2.4	1.2	2.1
Totals	13.2	11.7	8.8	10.6

Source: Estimates derived from New Earnings Survey and overall employment data.

Table 4: Overtime and Shiftwork Full-time Adult Employees
(April 1979 Survey)

	Manual		Non-Manual	
	Men	*Women*	*Men*	*Women*
Weekly				
Average Basic Hours	39.8	38.5	37.1	36.3
Average Overtime Hours	6.3	1.1	1.6	0.4
Total Average Hours	46.2	39.6	38.8	36.7
Overtime Pay as % of Average Earnings	15.0%	3.5%	3.5%	1.2%
Shift Premia as % of Average Earnings	3.2%	1.9%	0.6%	0.8%
THOSE RECEIVING OVERTIME PAY				
(in survey period)				
% of all Employees	58.5%	17.5%	20.3%	10.3%
Average Overtime Hours	10.6	6.1	7.2	4.0
Overtime Pay as % of Earnings	23.4%	16.4%	17.1%	11.1%
THOSE RECEIVING SHIFT PREMIA				
(in survey period)				
% of all Employees	23.6%	11.4%	5.6%	9.5%
Shift Premia as % of Average Earnings less Overtime Pay	14.1%	14.7%	11.6%	8.9%
Normal basic hours	39.4	38.7	38.5	38.9
Overtime Hours	7.4	2.0	5.0	0.6

Source: New Earnings Survey, 1979.

CHAPTER ELEVEN

European Unity:
A New Perspective

by Tony Benn

I want to examine Europe, divided between East and West, and then look much further ahead to new possibilities of co-operation that may exist for the future of our continent in the nineties and beyond. In brief, can we unite the whole of Europe in the next generation?

If Europe is to survive, and humanity is to be spared a nuclear holocaust, we *must* attempt that task. There must be fresh thinking, and a new agenda. The present division is symbolised by the Berlin Wall; on the one side the Communist countries under the influence of Moscow; on the other the West under the umbrella of America.

The two alliances, NATO and the Warsaw Pact, are both heavily armed with nuclear weapons, strategic, theatre and tactical — numbering between 10,000 and 15,000 missiles in position. Massive ground, air and naval forces are also deployed on both sides. Arms limitation talks, especially on SALT are deadlocked and arms expenditure is now planned to rise still further. The military establishment controlling these forces and this technology are funded on a large scale, command huge industrial resources, and are getting more and more powerful inside each nation that sustains them and, as a result, are getting harder and harder to control politically.

Meanwhile, in the background, the two superpowers have problems of their own which greatly influence their respective approaches to Europe. Mr Brezhnev is faced with a major revolt against Soviet domination in Poland, where working people are seeking greater democracy in their lives, and has sent troops into Afghanistan in an attempt to secure the southern flank against what he perceives to be infiltration. Who knows what other revolts lie under the surface in and around the USSR?

President Reagan is faced with a major revolt against American dominance in El Salvador, and is demanding the use of Western European troops in a NATO Rapid Deployment Force, to safeguard Western interests worldwide. Who knows what other revolts against US power lie under the surface in and around the USA?

Both the superpowers have their own interests in Europe but the division of our continent is not quite as sharp and clear as might be supposed.

Yugoslavia and Albania, each under a Communist government, stand apart from their neighbours in COMECON. The West is not monolithic either for, even allowing for further enlargement to include Spain and Portugal, the EEC does not include Sweden, Norway, Finland, Austria or Switzerland.

The complex pattern of European systems is a product of the past: The First World War, the Russian Revolution, the growth of Fascism, the Second Word War, and the subsequent tension which has persisted since.

The 1914-18 conflict derived from a clash of imperial interests. It inflicted serious damage on all the participants, and laid the foundation for much of what has happened since.

In 1920, the United States went into isolation, and the European economies, severely damaged by war, were thrown into slump and mass unemployment, which first brought Mussolini to power in Italy; then Hitler to power in Germany, Franco in Spain, Salazar in Portugal, and brought almost the whole of Europe under the control of the Nazis, from 1940 to 1945. The World War then brought the US back into Europe. It also encouraged great hopes for a new Europe amongst that generation — hopes which have never yet been realised.

The Russian Revolution has dominated the century as the French Revolution did in its time. It was a turning point in world history, and from then until now it has been the objective of various Western leaders to contain Soviet power or to overturn the régime itself. A British Expeditionary Force was sent to support the White Armies at Archangel in 1919. Twenty-two years later the German armies launched their blitzkrieg against the USSR, laying waste their territory and killing 25 million Russians. And as late as 17th April 1948 the American Ambassador in London, in a despatch to the US Secretary of State, reported on his talks with Winston Churchill in these words:

"He" — that is Churchill — "believes that now is the time, promptly, to tell the Soviet that if they do not retire from Berlin and abandon

Eastern Germany, withdrawing to the Polish frontier, we will raze their cities.''

It is necessary to remind ourselves of all these events in order to explain the developments of the last thirty years. For just as the West built up its defences under the American umbrella which gave birth to NATO; and built up its economies under the Marshall Plan and created the EEC; the Russians look to their defence system in terms of a *cordon sanitaire* of Communist states on their western border — including Eastern Germany — and established the Warsaw Pact to protect themselves from a fourth attack from the West.

The dominant factor in European politics today remains fear of attack by both East and West from each other. In the West, the Soviet control of East Germany, Czechoslovakia, Poland, Hungary, Bulgaria and Rumania, is widely interpreted as clear evidence of Soviet intentions to expand its control over the whole of Europe, and the military arsenals of the Warsaw Pact, with their heavy preponderance of ground troops, add to those fears. In Moscow the situation must look very different. Given Russia's past experience, the hostility of China, and the immense technical, industrial and economic superiority of the USA, the Kremlin calculates the balance of military forces on a different basis, which must look a great deal less favourable to them.

But the insecurity in American and Russia is not limited to their assessment of the external military threat as each sees it. For the Kremlin fears that the régimes in the Warsaw Pact countries would be unlikely to survive any genuine test of public opinion in a free election. And even at home, 64 years after the October Revolution, the repression of political opposition indicates that their system is still too vulnerable to survive the rigours of too much free debate. State Communism is still not willing to put itself to the proof of public support, that we would accept as democratic.

Nor is American without its own anxieties. The election of President Reagan suggests that millions of Americans sense and resent the evident decline of American power in the world — even close to home as in Latin America — and feel the need to assert themselves militarily to stop the rot. Will it lead to a US military adventure against Cuba just as a similar post-imperial crisis of self-confidence tempted Sir Anthony Eden into his attack on Egypt in 1956? Furthermore, the US is now in the grip of a massive economic recession which poses acute internal problems and is not the best possible advertisement for the virtues of capitalism. This slump is also affecting Western Europe.

Europe is therefore now caught up in the middle of this impasse between the superpowers, both of which show signs of being paralysed by their own deep sense of insecurity. But unless Europeans are content to remain pawns in a superpower chess game, we must seek to make our own judgements of what is happening, and why.

It is necessary for us first to consider whether we really believe the warnings that issue from Washington about Moscow's intentions; or from Moscow about Washington's plans.

My judgement is that both the Pentagon and the Kremlin are mistaken if they believe that the other is seriously planning for world domination. Each appear to be behaving exactly as Great Powers have always behaved — determined to safeguard their own homeland and vital interests; and seeking to extend their influence and interests and their ideology as far as they have the power to do so. That certainly was Britain's posture during the heyday of the Victorian Empire, and it even led Britain into an invasion of Afghanistan in the nineteenth century. But it is not credible to believe, in the age of nuclear weapons, that either superpower is preparing for expansion by war. And if either were to attempt it, by non-nuclear means, their plans would encounter such violent hostility world-wide and in the countries they occupied that they could not hope to succeed.

Some judgement of the intentions of the superpowers has to be made if Europe is to look to its own future in its own right. For as soon as we have cleared our own minds we can plan accordingly.

For those who believe that it is only a matter of time before the Red Army marches on the West, preceded by a bombardment from SS20 Missiles, then mass mobilisation, together with a crash programme of nuclear rearmament and civil defence measures, is the proper course. And if Russia really expects a direct attack on her security system she will activate her troops in Poland, establish military régimes in every Warsaw Pact country, and expand her nuclear weapons programme.

The reality is, of course, very different. Despite the renewal of the cold war and the escalation of the arms race, the real Europe does not behave as if it believed in the inevitability of war. Nor does the pattern of life in Europe, as it is, correspond at all with the rigid division between East and West which the superpower strategists seek to impose upon it in their speeches and writings.

This becomes clear as soon as any of the simple litmus paper tests are applied to the real world.

First, is it true that the conflict can be clarified in terms of ideology? Are we facing an holy war between "christian capitalism and atheistic communism''? Those who argue that case would have a difficult task to sustain it. There is too much evidence which points the other way.

Yugoslavia is a marxist state receiving political support from the West. In Poland the Church and the Communist Party have avoided confrontation, by accepting co-existence. Similarly, in the West, Marx has always been accepted as a towering socialist intellectual by most democratic socialist parties.

Many dissidents in Eastern Europe have denounced Stalinism on the grounds that it is a vicious distortion of the teachings of Marx. In Western Europe, the Communist Parties are no longer the monolithic blocs they were once thought to be. In Italy and Spain great changes have been made in organisational terms to allow more broad-based discussion, accepting political pluralism and rejecting the doctrine of the dictatorship proletariat. This is similar to the demands made in Gdansk last year, in the Prague Spring of 1968; and in Budapest in 1956.

No black and white division based on ideology stands up to examination. It would be truer to say that there is a growing demand for democracy in the Communist states, and for socialism in the states which accept parliamentary democracy.

The second untruth is that the Iron Curtain is impenetrable.

Look at the Ostpolitik of the Federal Republic of Germany and the human contacts that have been allowed. Look at the special relationship between Austria and Hungary that benefits both countries. These contacts are also developing in the Balkans.

Consider the pattern of trade between East and West. In 1978 Western Europe as a whole exported US $18 billion-worth of goods to Eastern Europe and imported US $£20 billion-worth in return. And in 1980, in spite of the increase in international tension intra-German trade remained high and profitable. Even in Energy, which is of vital importance to the world economy, Soviet gas exports and Polish coal exports to the West, though temporarily reduced, are a part of the economy of the real Europe and play an important role in its mutual prosperity. Europe needs an energy plan worked out, in detail, between East and West.

And, following the Helsinki Accords, there is growing contact in cultural matters and exchanges of visits and delegations, although they could be increased still further. The BBC World Service plays an important part in the process.

Many Western countries have technological agreements with the USSR and Eastern Europe. France pioneered them, then Germany, and I signed many of them myself as the British Minister of

Technology in the 1960s. Later, my own direct experience as Secretary of State with responsibility for nuclear matters taught me that there is even a close accord on the issue of proliferation of nuclear weapons, to which the Soviet Union is as strongly opposed as is the USA.

Even the denial of human rights is by no means confined to the Communist countries, as memories of Franco's Spain, Salazar's Portugal and today's Third World dictatorships, backed by the West, remind us. Europe is living together, and working together, and changing its prospects by doing so. The restoration of democracy in Portugal and Spain is very significant in this context. This is the reality to which we must turn our eyes.

Europe is a huge continent. Excluding the USSR, the traditional Europe consists of twenty-nine countries; ten in the EEC; eleven outside the EEC and eight in COMECON. Its total area is nearly 6 million square kilometres and its total population is over 500 million. Together, its national income added up in 1978 to US $27,700 billion.

The present institutional framework within which today's Europe works is complex. In the West there is the Council of Europe, the EEC and EFTA, NATO and the OECD, and the Nordic Council. In the East COMECON and the Warsaw Pact. But that is not all. The UN has its own Regional Commission, set up after the last war. The United Nations Economic Commission for Europe is, however, concerned with both East and West. But, like the UN itself, its role has been ignored or downgraded in the West.

To speak of the continent as a whole will be so strange to the ears of many people, and to consider plans for its future, in co-operation, may seem visionary at this moment. But, despite all that has happened, there is a strong common interest on which to build.

The surest starting point must be the demonstrable desire of all the people of Europe for the achievement of certain minimum necessities of life itself. The people of Poland, like the people of Portugal; or the inhabitants of the two Germanies; or of Britain and Czechoslovakia — must necessarily hope and pray for peace for themselves and their families. Everyone wants work and good housing, health care and adequate schooling, opportunities for the young, dignity in retirement, and a fair distribution of wealth.

The majority would like to enjoy full human rights and political and trade union freedom so that they can organise and express themselves openly and without fear of victimisation. Women want equality and ethnic and cultural minorities want safeguards. Everybody would prefer to live in circumstances which allow them a real say over those who govern them. And the demand for regional self-determination is to be found in many countries.

Unfortunately, nowhere in Europe today are *all* these rights achieved or aspirations met. But for anyone who seeks to uphold these rights it is clear that there is a strong common interest amongst common people in détente and disarmament than in tension and the arms race. If that is all true — and it is so obvious as to be beyond argument — we have to turn our minds to those policies which might move us towards their realisation.

Any serious attempt to identify such policies must begin with the problems of security. Every government, of whatever political complexion, always makes security its first priority. That was the foundation upon which both the League of Nations and the United Nations based their Charters.

We must then ask ourselves how that security is to be achieved, and whether the balance of nuclear terror satisfies that requirement. I cite only one witness on this issue: Lord Mountbatten, a Supreme Commander of World War II, who, just before his death, delivered a remarkable lecture on this very subject. Speaking at the Stockholm International Peace Research Institute on 11th May 1979, Mountbatten said:

"As a military man who has given half a century of military service, I say in all sincerity that the nuclear arms race has no military purpose. Wars cannot be fought with nuclear weapons. Their existence only adds to our perils because of the illusions which they have generated.

There are powerful voices around the world who still give credence to the old Roman precept — 'If you desire peace, prepare for war'. This is absolute nuclear nonsense, and I repeat — it is a disastrous misconception to believe that by increasing the total uncertainty one increases one's own certainty."

A growing number of Europe's half-billion population would share that judgement, and I am one of them.

How can we reverse the drift to nuclear war?

The most hopeful initiative that has emerged in Europe has been the growing demand for European Nuclear Disarmament to make our whole continent a nuclear-free zone. It has been canvassed by ministers over the years in both East and West, in speeches by Poles, Czechs and East Germans. The Irish Government touched on it in 1959 and the Swedes and Finns have also promoted it. Last year the European Nuclear Disarmament Movement began to gather momentum in West Europe, including Britain, and an appeal for support was launched in several capitals, and it has met with an encouraging response.

This groundswell of opinion is growing as the arms race threatens to grow. It would be a mistake to present this argument in terms of pacifism. For many who are not pacifists now see nuclear weapons as a recipe for mass destruction and not as a defence policy at all. Others — like the British Labour Party — have decided to oppose all military strategies based upon the threat or use of nuclear weapons, and favour a non-nuclear defence policy, rejecting Trident, and Cruise Missiles, and the deployment of the Neutron bomb. We want a defence policy that would defend our homeland and its people, not one which threatens to obliterate it. Here is a campaign which really does offer a future with some hope instead of the acceptance of fear as the main driving force for security.

Moreover, experience since 1945 strongly suggests — as Vietnam and Algeria established, and Afghanistan and Poland may prove yet again — that a determined people is the best guarantee against permanent domination from outside. Decisions about peace and war cannot be subcontracted to a man in a bomb-proof shelter with control over a nuclear button.

The Swedes and the Swiss have certainly founded their defence strategy upon ''dissuasion'' rather than ''deterrence'' and it makes a lot more sense to examine that option carefully. Both have a large citizen army that can be mobilised very quickly and would inflict immense casualties on any invader, without nuclear weapons or creating a military élite that could organise a domestic coup.

But security is not entirely an external problem. Internal security must necessarily rest in the end upon a foundation of popular consent. For example, the French Revolution with its battle cry ''Liberty, Equality and Fraternity'', overthrew the *Ancien Régime* of the Bourbons, which did not enjoy that consent.

The appeal for popular support for Socialism was defined in 1848 in these words:

''The free development of each is the condition for the free development of all.''

And in El Salvador in July 1980 Pope John Paul said:

''Any society which does not wish to be destroyed from within must establish a just social order.''

These beliefs, and the commitment to achieve them, inspired the British trade unions, when they demanded the vote for the working class in Britain more than a hundred years ago, just as the Polish trade unions have raised the same cry today. And it is the same voices from the Third World which are now demanding social justice and a new world economic order through UN.

The achievement of domestic justice and domestic security is a great deal easier when no external threat can be used as an excuse for internal repression. That too points to the desirability of détente, rather than a nuclear arms race. It also points to the importance of stimulating trade and commerce between East and West, and seeking to interlock the economies of the two blocks so tightly that interdependence makes conflict increasingly difficult and ultimately impossible. In this context we have to decide whether it is in our interests in the West for the economy of Eastern Europe to fail or to succeed. In the world we live in we have now a powerful interest in our mutual economic success, even if only to reduce the likelihood that any government, East or West, may be tempted to divert domestic discontent towards some foreign enemy and thus hope to retain public support.

But if co-operation *is* to be achieved, how and where could we begin to discuss it?

There is one body which we could revive. The United Nations Economic Commission for Europe, an agency with precisely the mandate we need. Delegations to its conference could, and should, be raised to ministerial level, and made into a major forum for developing Pan-European co-operation. Into that framework the proposals made by Mr Brezhnev for high level East/West conferences on transport, energy, and the environment, could be made real. At least it would be a start, and could consolidate the many bilateral agreements which exist.

But to be effective, contact must also be strengthened at all non-governmental levels. Western businessmen have never allowed ideological differences to inhibit their search for markets as the East/West trade figures show, and Western multinational corporations have signed many agreements with state trading corporations from the East. But the formal division of the Trade Union Movement world-wide remains much as it was when the World Federation of Trade Unions broke up at the height of the cold war. There are, in fact, 4,500 separate trade unions in the whole of Europe — 3,000 of them in one country, Greece. Allowing for the quite different trade union role in Communist and non-Communist countries, there are, in total, 105 million members of the trade unions in Europe as a whole.

Trade union delegations travel regularly between East and West, but there is no Pan-European trade union organisational forum at which the role of trade unions can be discussed. Yet the concern of the unions in the West at the re-emergence of mass unemployment, and the possibility that "Solidarity" in Poland may trigger off parallel demands for free trade unionism in the COMECON countries — and there is already some evidence of this — suggests that it would be in the interests of trade unions in the East and West to institute more regular and structured discussions.

Finally — and most important of all — we must supplement the present East/West cultural exchanges by encouraging a real political dialogue. The blanket acceptance that no dialogue on politics, ideology or religion could be meaningful is a by-product of cold war thinking. Yet the issues which concern us all must necessarily lead us in this direction.

Politics is not *just* about personalities, parties or policies. It is about institutions and, above all, about values. In Latin America the liberation theology has brought priests, trade unionists and socialists into a close alliance of thought and action against poverty and repression. Europeans, East and West, should now have enough courage and faith to attempt to sort out some of its problems by engaging in a similar dialogue in a forum created for that purpose.

If such a future is to be sought how do we get from here to there? What will happen to the European Community, to EFTA and to COMECON? Prophecy is a risky occupation, especially for those who are active in politics. Moreover, the existing institutional framework is well established and cannot easily be dismantled or quickly transformed. Yet there are already signs of pressure for change from within both East and West.

The peoples of Eastern Europe will not forever accept their present role under the tutelage of Moscow, with internal bureaucracies claiming the right to govern. Rising living standards, better education and the emergence of a generation born after 1945, which does not remember the past, must necessarily lead to growing demands for liberalisation and democratic rights. Though the remnants of Stalinism hold few attractions for them, there is no reason to suppose that this new generation wants to reinstate capitalism, let alone the right-wing military Governments which existed in some Eastern European states in pre-war days. This process is to be welcomed so long as it is a natural growth from within the countries concerned.

But, if attempts are made from the outside to exploit these developments explicitly to destabilise Eastern Europe or to weaken Soviet security in the sense that John Foster Dulles once threatened to 'liberate' Eastern Europe, the attempt to introduce democracy and self-government could end in tragedy for them — and for us.

State communism and its international system must be transformed from the inside and it is in our interests to allow that to happen. These internal reforms are much more likely to succeed if they can take place within a framework of growing European co-operation and détente, and without raising the spectre of a security threat for the Russians which their military leaders might then use as an excuse for intervention.

But pressure for internal reform is not confined to Eastern Europe. The Western economies are stagnating with high and chronic unemployment and cut-backs in essential services. There are today, eight-and-a-half million unemployed in the EEC; and allowing for two dependents in every household, this means that nearly twenty-five million people in the Common Market are now living in homes where the breadwinner is out of work and the family income is dependent upon Social Benefits, the real value of which may be eroded by inflation. Even this leaves out of account the special problems of women, who have have been hardest hit by unemployment, and those who are suffering from a fall in income through short-time working and the pressure to cut health, housing and education, which affects everyone.

The European Trade Union Confederation in its indicative full employment plan for the Western European economy as a whole for 1980-1985, estimates the cost of unemployment — in lost production now — to be 75 billion European units of account. The Confederation calls for nearly 15 million new jobs to be created by 1985 if unemployment is to be reduced to 2% in that year.

In the 1930s it was unemployment which paved the way for Fascism and it was Public Expenditure in the form of rearmament that ended the slump and brought back full employment. The challenge to this generation is how to return to full employment without rearmament and war.

It is against this background that the whole philosophy of the Treaty of Rome which entrenches and sanctifies market forces will now be judged. The most telling critique of that Treaty which is now emerging is not based upon national interests but upon its inherent defects and the undemocratic nature of the Commission itself, which operate against the true interests of the peoples in all member states.

As the Community changes by enlargement — or withdrawal — the pressure for a much looser and wider association of fully self-governing states in Europe is likely to be canvassed and could transform the whole nature of European co-operation in the West. Moreover, as the EEC needs to import a great deal of its energy, the necessity for links with Norway, with the USSR and Poland and with OPEC, all outside the EEC, suggests a less self-sufficient posture than has been attempted in, say, agriculture. If the people in the COMECON countries moved to greater democracy, people in the EEC will be moving by democracy towards greater social planning combined with greater decentralisation and social accountability as well.

These concurrent political movements will necessitate greater flexibility in both parts of Europe, and with a common interest between East and West developing simultaneously, new institutions for Europe as a whole could possibly be constructed to accommodate and assist the convergence of systems towards democracy and socialism.

It may be too soon to think of the summoning of a Pan-European Peoples' Congress to allow this work to begin. But at some stage a real "Council of Continental Europe" will need to be brought together and ultimately its representatives should be directly elected to provide a true forum in which the future of Europe can be discussed. And when that is achieved it must be seen as a part of a United Nations strategy upon which our hopes for World peace must necessarily depend.

A whole generation of young people put their faith in the United Nations at the end of the last World War and the revival of the United Nations role is of critical importance at this period in our history. Nothing less will be able to cement the sort of shared understanding world-wide, reached through dialogue, upon which a secure and peaceful Europe must necessarily rebuild its confidence.

We are a continent with an ancient civilisation and history, rich with resources, human, material and mineral, including coal, oil and gas. We have a highly skilled people with well established agriculture and industries. We have many religions, Catholic and Protestant, Jews and Moslems, and a rich tradition of political thought, including Humanists, Socialists, Liberals, Conservatives and Marxists. We have suffered grievously in war, and we are having to learn once more that we must live together, or die together.

This, then, is a draft agenda for discussing a New Europe that would be really worth working to build.

We need talks about security, European nuclear disarmament; more co-operation in trade, technology and energy under UN auspices — all supplemented by a real political dialogue that brings working people together.

It is not to soon to begin thinking about Europe in the 21st Century which lies less than 19 years ahead. Our vision must be of Peace, Jobs and Freedom, achieved between fully self-governing states within a security system ultimately replacing both the Warsaw Pact and NATO. We must envisage a multi-polar world, well disposed to America and Russia, but under the control of neither. Europe must play a full part in the UN to realise the aims of its Charter, respect the demands for self-determination and independence in Third World countries with whom we must establish a constructive dialogue.

It is a vision for our children and our children's children, and in that spirit I commend it for consideration.

I offer you a text for tomorrow's Europe. It comes from Mahatma Ghandhi, whose advocacy of non-violence makes him a fitting prophet for today.

> "I do not want my house to be walled in on all sides nor my windows to be shut.
>
> "I want the culture of all lands to blow about my house, as freely as possible, but I refuse to be blown off my feet by any of them."

A Postscript: on the Social Democrats

We began by pointing out that the British Press in spite of its almost general wish to bring aid and sympathy to the Government, has found it impossible to avoid registering the disastrous scale of present unemployment.

At the same time, counterpointing the dismal figures and terrifying prognoses, there flit through the pages of our newspapers ghosts of a former time, in the shapes of Roy Jenkins, David Owen and Shirley Williams. Co-architects of significant parts of our present mess, these wraiths now sing out boldly for the merits of yesterday. It is not exactly surprising that yesterday suits them, because it afforded them notable comforts, a certain prestige, and a platform from which to denounce tomorrow. They may indeed be right, that tomorrow will be awful. If it is, they will have made an inimitable contribution to that as well. If it is not, it will be because the working men and women of our country, and those many millions who wish for work but are denied it, have found their way past the beguiling arts of demagogy, and begun to engage directly, on their own account, with the gruelling problems which confront them.

In order to do this we must look a little carefully at the relationship between unemployment and modern "social democracy". We must also look at the scope for industrial democracy which has suffered so considerably at the hands of self-proclaimed social democrats, and which yet remains our most powerful potential resource for recovery.

*   *   *

"Between the wars unemployment in Great Britain never fell below 750,000. It averaged 1,650,000 and, for a short time, at the beginning of 1933, it rose to more than 3,000,000. These facts dominated the approach of the Labour Party to home politics during the whole of the period."[1]

That was how Roy Jenkins began his postwar assessment of Labour experience and doctrine in his book *Pursuit of Progress,* published in 1953. But what was the contemporary response to such facts? It was summed up in one book which could represent hundreds of others which appeared in the 'thirties: C.R. Attlee's *The Labour Party in Perspective.* This, Mr Jenkins was to write, a decade and a half later, "said some things which now sound very odd indeed". These things were the conventional pre-war socialist response to crisis. To recall them will afford us a measure of the remarkably temperate mood of the contemporary Labour movement.

"All the major industries" Attlee had assumed when sketching the framework of his future socialist commonwealth, "will be owned and controlled by the community" even while small enterprises could be "carried on individually". There would be significant devolution of power by regional decentralisation. In order to speedily establish effective planning for the creation of work where it was needed, and to produce useful goods which could be more equally distributed, a Labour Government would seek a specific mandate to override opposition from the House of Lords. It would not brook delay in its necessary measures, and would therefore deal far more resolutely with the peers than had the Liberals during their constitutional crisis, because, unlike them, it would be "in the business of transforming society".[2]

Attlee at that time was what is today called a "moderate". Others were far more radical. Much of what Sir Stafford Cripps was writing at the same time would nowadays be regarded as "extreme" by the majority of the leftwing delegates to Labour Party Conferences. Between Attlee and Cripps the entire Labour Party, by 1937, had come to occupy ground whose topography looks not altogether unfamiliar to those seeking bearings in 1981.

In 1981 unemployment is almost universally expected to pass the 3,500,000 mark. Many forecasters anticipate a level of 4,000,000. Our crisis is already deeper than that which formed the background to Attlee's assumption of the Labour leadership. Not only is it deeper, but it is also manifestly more intractable.

In this extremity, whatever they may have said or done when the International Monetary Fund revoked the electoral commitments of the Callaghan administration, present-day Labour leaders, so they say, all favour an alternative economic strategy. The net package of proposals which Labour has been discussing under this genial rubric throughout this more recent period is certainly not less measured than was Attlee's book in 1937, to say nothing of the contemporary writings of Strachey or Laski. Yet it is at just this moment that Roy Jenkins, Shirley Williams and David Owen, with a cohort of more pedestrian public figures, have resolved to turn against the Labour movement because of its alleged intransigence and to form a new party based on the cult of moderation. This will uphold, they claim, the principles of social democracy.

Social democracy has, like many other political currents, an ambiguous history. The first English practitioners of the creed were, on the while, a somewhat pious, not to say tedious, bunch of doctrinaires, who formed the Social Democratic Federation around a remarkable eccentric, H.M. Hyndman. They preached a plagiarised and repetitious marxism, not greatly more simple-minded than the cliches of the vigorously traduced Militant Group in the present Labour Party. They were affiliated to the Party for many years, although for most of this time their influence was hardly electric. In Europe, Lenin and Trotsky and Luxemburg and Liebknecht and Kautsky and Bernstein, Pannekoek and Cachin were also social democrats all, until the 1914 war tore the continental Labour movement into warring schisms. But in Britain, Lee and Archbold apart, social democrats only re-emerged as a visible entity in the years after the Second World War. Old social democrats sought to extend democratic controls to every aspect of industrial and social life. New social democrats had rather less taxing aspirations. That is why most Labour people still claimed allegiance to one or another variant of "socialism", as did Richard Crossman in 1951, when he tried to explain the Party's worsening electoral fortunes in a characteristically imaginative way:

> "The socialist's greatest achievement is that he has made the working class in this country forget what it felt like to be afraid of unemployment and so become full of grievances which were previously the monopoly of a prosperous upper class".[3]

This is a poor thought: but in times of intellectual austerity it was rapidly taken up and developed. In its elaboration there arose the school of self-styled social democrats of the later '50s, with which Roy Jenkins himself was closely associated.

Superficially, the establishment of relatively full employment in a predominantly unchanged capitalist economy could be taken as a refutation of Attlee's "socialist objective". Of course, man does not live by bread alone, but moral needs are often more difficult to assert than physical ones. This is no excuse for those of Labour's ideologues who persistently reduced their estimates of their fellows' needs to a mess of pottage. Cutting deeper, Attlee's objectives might have been revised to develop their expressed antipathy to wage-slavery and subordination, as indeed R.H. Tawney himself suggested, in his last major political essay.

> "If a socialist government means business — if it intends to create an economic system socialist all through, and not merely at the top — then it should use the industries in public ownership as a laboratory where different methods of making industrial democracy a reality are tested ..."[4]

These were words of good counsel, partly, but only partly, diluted when their author continued:

> there should be a systematic attempt to democratise the practical routine of industrial life by transferring to bodies representing the wage-earners such functions as the allocation of jobs within a working group; the appointment of leaders in charge of them; and matters relating to promotion, dismissal and disciplinary procedures."[5]

In truth this remained a modest programme, but Tawney's self-avowed disciples were almost all persistently deaf to it. For them, all such autonomy in the workforce was contrary to the natural order of things, so that trade unions had to struggle hard, and against relentless official opposition, for even the smallest gains in their members' practical status, whether those in power were "social democrats" or not.

The general lesson drawn from near full employment by these philosophers was precisely opposed to Tawney's fundamental insight. Since public ownership was for them inconceivable outside the bureaucratic forms imposed under Herbert Morrison's model of the London Passenger Transport Board, then public ownership itself was seen as an electoral liability. Full employment was enough, as far as could or should be reached or even attempted in the scale of social transformation. What remained for social democrats was to administer it humanely. Humanity itself became a shrinking concept within this view. C.A.R. Crosland, who was in many ways the most sympathetic of the grouping, nonetheless took Tawney's call for experiments in workplace industrial democracy at their least possible value, and then shrivelled them without mercy:

> "the problem is basically one of 'democratic participation' — not however, the mass participation of *all* workers in the *higher* management, but the participation of the *primary* work group in deciding how its *own* work should be divided, organised and remunerated".[6]

We should notice that Tawney had moved from the general to the particular: from the ideal to a practical proposal. Crosland, by contrast, here starts in the particular, apparently not far away from Tawney. But then see how, in his next sentence, he reaches for the general idea:

> On this view, we must study the enterprise as a social organism, unravel the natural group relationships, *and endeavour to align these with the technological necessities of the work process."*[7] (my emphasis).

Big Brother is watching you. If Tawney was listening, he might well have screamed.

Clearly it is not easy to persuade people that "alignment" of this kind is an exciting or satisfying mode of life, leave alone a "socialist objective". When they do it to battery hens or veal calves, societies protest about it.

Yet Crosland was close to the truth, in a limited way, as well as the consensus of of his time, when he spoke of "the sellers' market for labour" which full employment created, as transferring a degree of effective social power to working people.

In our previous book *What Went Wrong,* I cited the seminal text of social democracy in the 1950s, *Twentieth Century Socialism,* on this consensus. Written by Allan Flanders and Rita Hinden, and representing the views of the journal *Socialist Commentary* directly, and the opinions of Hugh Gaitskell indirectly, this little book was published by Penguin in 1956. Here was its cardinal tenet:

> "Planning for economic security means, first and foremost, planning to maintain full employment. Socialists can admit no compromise with this aim, no scaling it down to 'a high and stable level of employment', no playing with the idea that 'a small dose of unemployment' might be good for production. Just as the certainty of a job is the first condition of decent living, so is full employment the first condition of a socialist economy. Even if it could be proved conclusively — and all the evidence points in the opposite direction — that a revival of the fear of unemployment would increase productivity, this would be a poor bargain and a disgraceful exchange."[8]

This was the shared conviction of all the social democrats of the revisionist vintage, whether, like Douglas Jay, they were to remain part of the Labour movement, or like Roy Jenkins, they were subsequently to set up in opposition to it. Even so, it was not a conviction strong enough to prevent them from ulcerating their stomachs in the cause of reducing or subverting that social power which Crosland celebrated, when they were to come to office in the Wilson and subsequent Callaghan administrations. Denied any democratic conquests of industrial significance, workpeople naturally used their "sellers' market", such as it was, to maximise their earnings, such as they were. They were thus identified as causes of inflationary pressure. Every governmental ingenuity was therefore deployed to curb their exploitation of such advantages as they might otherwise have derived from this favourable situation.

Happily, such curbs worked far from perfectly, and the reason was that while full employment made far less fundamental changes than could easily have been achieved in the organisation of work, it did greatly strengthen and consolidate some of the processes of political democracy. In this context it wrestled from authority some serious advances in public welfare, and paradoxically went a long way towards giving the modern social democratic platform of "Butskellism" as it became called, the semblance of justification.

Yet these gains were all allowed to slide into jeopardy when the 1974-9 Labour Governments chose a series of policy options which reneged upon the "first and foremost" priority of *Twentieth Century Socialism,* flouting the "first condition of a socialist economy" and thus entering into "a disgraceful exchange". We documented the drift into this morass in *What Went Wrong,* in a detailed essay by Francis Cripps and Frances Morrell. Mr Jenkins and his three co-responsible companions can have it one way: if the Labour Government made such a "disgraceful exchange" with conscious forethought then it was reneging on exactly that social democracy which they claim as their very own tradition. Or they can have it another way, protesting their lack of any such villainy, and claiming with those defenders of the Callaghan regime who have remained in the Labour Party, that vast impersonal economic convulsions deprived them of any choice in the matter. In this case, they are claiming that the social conditions which gave rise to social democracy have disappeared. If this be so, then the relevance of the doctrine has also disappeared.

In fact, they seem to make a third claim, which is that social democracy is to do with abstract moderation, and that by implication Flanders, Crosland, Hinden and everyone else were totally unjustified in linking it to such impolite matters as the right to work. Some people still think that to be moderate in the face of rank injustice, such as mass unemployment, is an ignoble response, but no doubt there are persons in Oxford or at the BBC who will explain to them that it is necessary to maintain an impartial detachment between good and evil. Naturally, such matters are not discussed very loudly in social democratic meetings. Instead, there are lusty invocations on the merits of yesterday. And yes, yesterday was more comfortable than today.

Certainly, if we could go back, three million workless people would opt like a shot for the apparent stability of the full employment years, however little they might offer in spiritual fulfilment and human dignity. It is an impossible "if" though. There is no going back. Far from moving into industrial (and therefore also "social") democracy, we shall quickly see our political freedoms themselves all shredded if full employment is not restored. And the old consensus cannot even promise to halve the queues at the Labour Exchanges, leave alone remove them. It is not at all excluded that it would, given the opportunity, actually increase them. It is hauntingly obvious that a modest recovery in economic fortunes would stimulate labour-saving investment which might waste more jobs than it secured. Already, as a result of the present crisis, tensions rise, old and young come into bitter conflict, racial disharmony becomes more sinister, the police are armed with ever more elaborate weapons, and authoritarian trends become daily more ominous. The process is clearly visible.

Against all this, the social democrats of all parties offer no hope. Not one of them has offered any beginning of a plausible suggestion about how to restore full employment. Reflation, as a measure taken alone, will suck in vast imports from the EEC whilst only marginally admitting industrial growth. Protection is still abjured, leave alone the planning of trade, which is the only rational response. The spokesmen of the old order, whether they sport new colours or not, are all tacitly united in assuming permanent mass unemployment. This means civil dislocation and stress at unbearable levels, and it can only be policed by the abandonment of every liberal precept which has been established in the postwar era. And at the end of it all, as the oil dries out, lies open bankruptcy. It is not imaginable that the British people will tolerate this dreadful prospectus, when they understand it for what it really is.

This book offers an attempt to chart a different path.

References

1. Roy Jenkins: *Pursuit of Progress — A critical analysis of the achievement and prospect of the Labour Party,* Heinemann, 1953, p.55.
2. C.R. Attlee: *The Labour Party in Perspective,* Gollancz (Left Book Club), 1937, p.153 *et seq.*
3. R.H.S. Crossman: *Socialist Values in a Changing Situation,* Fabian Tract No. 286, 1951.
4. R.H. Tawney: *The Radical Tradition,* Penguin Books, 1966, p.185.
5. *Ibid.,* p.186.
6. C.A.R. Crosland: 'What the Worker Wants', *Encounter,* February 1959, p.17.
7. *Ibid.*
8. Allan Flanders and Ruth Hinden: *Twentieth Century Socialism,* Penguin Books, 1956, p.66.